201 Things You Need To Know About Life

Before It's Too Late

201 Things You Need To Know About Life

Before It's Too Late

Thomas R Morris

Simple Logic Publications

201 Things You Need To Know About Life

Copyright © 2021 Thomas R. Morris All rights reserved. No part of this book may be reproduced or transmitted by any means or in any form without the prior written consent from the author or publisher. This includes photocopying, scanning, storing in or transmitting by any computer-based device or system.

Disclaimer: This book has been created for general reference and is intended merely to provide thoughts regarding the subject matter covered. This book is sold with the full understanding that the publisher and author are not engaged in rendering advice of any kind. The publisher and author make no representations or warranties of any kind with respect to this book or its contents. The publisher and author make no guarantees concerning the outcome or results arising out of or in connection with this book and disclaim any and all liability for any damages arising out of or in connection with this book. Use of this book or its content is at the reader's own risk.

Talk with your doctor before starting any exercise program.

ISBN 978-0-9954007-3-3 (Trade Paperback)

For information, please contact the publisher at:
information@simplelogicpublications.com

Illustrations under license from istockphoto.com, adobe.com and shutterstock.com

Printed in Australia • United Kingdom
• United States of America

211022

Table of Contents

Introduction 1

Part 1 You 3

Part 2 Health 19

Part 3 Work Money Success 31

Part 4 Relationships 47

Part 5 Happiness 61

Part 6 Life in General 75

Epilogue 115

Things to Read 117

BONUS 40 More Things 133
           (Including Sex)

Quotes and Sources

1 François Rochefoucauld
2 Buddha
3 Chinese Proverb
4 Plutarch
5 Victor Hugo
6 Ralph Waldo Emerson
7 Harvard Medical School
8 www.mayoclinic.org
9 American Cancer Society
10 Confucius
11 Ralph Waldo Emerson
12 Thomas Edison
13 Henry David Thoreau
14 Democritus
15 Mark Twain
16 Benjamin Franklin
17 Buddha
18 Ralph Waldo Emerson
19 Aristotle
20 Lucius Annaeus Seneca
21 Marcus Aurelius
22 Rudolf Steiner
23 Alexander the Great
24 Confucius
25 Epictetus
26 Marcus Aurelius
27 Edgar Allan Poe
28 Mark Twain
29 Chinese Proverb
30 Aesop
31 Abraham Lincoln
32 Marcus Aurelius
33 Leonardo da Vinci
34 Chinese Proverb
35 John Pym
36 Horace
37 Lao Tzu
38 Chinese Proverb
39 Johann Wolfgang von Goethe
40 Michelangelo
41 Vincent van Gogh
42 Epictetus
43 Ralph Waldo Emerson
44 Johann Wolfgang von Goethe
45 Lucius Annaeus Seneca
46 Henry David Thoreau
47 Ralph Waldo Emerson
48 Epictetus
49 Francis Bacon
50 Abraham Lincoln
51 Alexander Graham Bell
52 Confucius
53 Victor Hugo

Introduction

Life is short and it gets shorter each day. Chances are it's the only life we get. Some of us will have 80 plus years to live life. For others, it may be far less. Life is wonderful, and there is so much we can do in life.

Government and big business constantly tell us what we need to do or have in order to live life the way we are *supposed* to live it or to be happy. Society applies pressure on us to fit in, to be and act like everyone else. And family and friends may try to convince us who and what we *should* be and how to live our life.

You don't want other people to determine how you live your life. You don't want to live life just like everyone else. And you don't want to settle for a life that's not right for you. Do you?

The life of your dreams is out there. You simply need the *right* information, knowledge and how-to skills, and to do what you need to do to get and live it. The *sooner* you have it and the earlier you get started, the greater your chances are of getting and living the life you dream of living.

Creating and living the life of your dreams is a *Do-It-Yourself* project. You can't sit back and expect your life to happen the way you want it to happen. You can't expect other people to make your life happen how you want it to happen. You need to make things happen the way you want things to happen. The time to start is now.

This book sets out 201 things that may help you to get and live the life you really want. The 201 things in this book aren't difficult. They simply need to be read, understood and acted on.

Before you do get started, it's important to understand the difference between *subjective* and *objective*. Put simply: Being subjective means *interpreting* what things are and mean based on or influenced by beliefs, biases, feelings, emotions, opinions and perception. Being objective means seeing and thinking of things as they *really are*, based solely on facts verifiable by proof.

Being *objective* when acquiring knowledge, making important decisions, and doing things that could have an impact on your health, happiness, safety or life – is likely to make life happier and better. It's also likely to get you where you want to be with fewer setbacks and less emotional or mental distress. It can be difficult to be objective. However, if you ask yourself if you're *being objective*, you're likely to be more objective than not.

PART 1
YOU

What lies behind you and what lies in front of you, pales in comparison to what lies inside of you.

Ralph Waldo Emerson

1

We are: who we think we are, who we think others think we are, who we are tying to convince and want others to think we are, and who we really are. They're not the same person. The first three are subjective, the fourth is objective. Take an objective look at yourself to determine who you really are. Once you know who that is, *take action* to adjust, improve and change the things about yourself that are stopping you from becoming and being who you truly wish to be.

2

One of the toughest things in life may be deciding who we really want to be. *Trust yourself* to decide who that will be. Disregard what others may have told you who you can and can't be. Take the time to discover who you truly wish to be. Think about the things you admire in those you respect and in those you aspire to be. Daydream without limits on who you can dream of being. Think about what truly excites you and what makes you truly happy. Then determine what you need to do to become who you decided you really want to be and do something each day toward becoming that person.

3

It's a waste of your time and life trying to be like other people. *Be yourself*. Discover who you really are; your beliefs, values and perspective on things. Think about your attitude and personality – what you think, how you behave and how you feel about things. *Recognize* your weaknesses and work on them to *become a better you*. It can be difficult and can take a lot of courage to be yourself (to be different from others), but doing so gives you the opportunity to become someone you are truly happy to be.

4

We are so accustomed to disguise ourselves to others that in the end we become disguised to ourselves.[1]
Many of us unknowingly wear *masks* to hide our insecurities, to fit in or to appear to be someone other than ourselves. It may be the tough or cool guy/gal mask (the way we walk, talk or dress) or the successful mask (the car we drive). By wearing masks, we may fool ourselves into believing that we are someone we aren't. This can stop us from overcoming our insecurities and from becoming who we are pretending to be or wish to be. Recognize the masks you wear and step out from behind them and fix what needs fixing.

5

How you define things, the rules you attached to things and the standards that you apply to things all play a major role in who you become and what you do and get in life. These definitions, rules and standards are a part of who you are. They are what your choices, decisions and goals are based on. They determine what you will and won't accept from others and life. They can get you or stop you from getting what you want in life. Know what your definitions, rules and standards are and adjust or change any that don't represent who you want to be, do or get.

6

Some or many of your current beliefs, values and principles were created during your childhood. This means that some *are likely to be* those of your parents (which may be outdated, wrong or not right for you, or could be stopping you from being who you want to be living the life you want). Beliefs, values and principles play an important role in and influence the things you do in your life. To become who you want to be and to get what you want in life, you need to question your beliefs, values and principles and make adjustments and changes where needed.

7

The first rule of self-defense is – if confronted by someone who aims to harm you, walk or run away and fight only if it's the only option. Regardless of how tough you are, the other person might be tougher, might be armed, could cause you serious injury or may later seek revenge. You need to know *how to defend yourself*. Knowing how to do so gives you the skills and confidence to defend yourself in the event that you need to. You don't need to earn a black belt in a martial art. A basic self-defense class with practice should do the trick.

8

Never be afraid to admit: you don't know, you made a mistake, you are sorry, or you need help. If we don't acknowledge these things, we won't take steps to gain information, fix or correct mistakes or things we have done, or get help. If we don't do so, we can't and won't be able to improve ourselves. New information, simple corrections or small improvements, apologizing when an apology is due and asking for help when help is needed can lead to great improvements in ourselves and in our life.

9

We all make mistakes. It would be a greater mistake not to learn from them. Learn what you can so that you don't make the same mistake again. Fix the things you can, let go of the things you can't and move on. Learn from the mistakes of others. This can save you the time, energy and pain of experiencing it for yourself. Ask people who have made the mistakes you wish to avoid how they made those mistakes. (A bad marriage or career choice, or not saving enough money for retirement are important examples.)

10

Being bold may be more important than being smart when it comes to getting what you really want in life. Being *bold* means sounding and appearing like you know what you're saying and doing (confident). It also means being forward, daring, unafraid of risk or difficult situations, and in control. Being bold doesn't mean being arrogant, rude, reckless or forceful. Being bold is about having the *nerve to ask for* what you want, going after what you want and not accepting anything less than what you ask for. By being bold, chances are people will give you what you want and you will get what you are after.

11

You will fail, a number of times (we all do and will). Accept and learn from your failures but *never be comfortable/OK with failure*. Failure should be a learning experience, a lesson on how not to do something or how to do something right or better next time. Being uncomfortable or not OK often motivates us to do something about that discomfort. Being comfortable or OK with failure can lead to complacency or acceptance of failing. Both can stop us from learning and thus stopping ourselves from making our life better.

12

Being able to stand up and effectively and confidently speak in front of others can enable us to get more of what we want in life. Knowing how to present ourselves verbally can be a useful and valuable asset in many areas of life. It may be when buying a car, presenting an idea at work, speaking with politicians to change current policy or even defending ourselves in court. Take a class or two in public speaking. The skills and experience will give you the confidence you need to effectively speak to people or even hundreds of people without being intimidated or afraid. People listen to people who appear confident.

13

No one likes a *Dickhead*. (Being a dickhead isn't just a guy thing. Girls too can be dickheads.) Aim to be a realistic, considerate, respectful, caring and mindful person. Be responsible, honest and fair. Be authentic and remember your manners. Give others the chance to say what they want to say and listen to and be polite in response to what they have to say. If you don't know or if you aren't really sure what a dickhead is, then you should read the book *Are You A Dickhead?* by Fred Mogura.

14

What you think you become.[2] Be a positive person; have a *positive attitude*. Having a positive attitude means thinking and acting in a positive way. It's about being *optimistic* not pessimistic; your glass being half-full not half-empty. It means focusing on the bright side of life and expecting that things will work out, even when things are not the way you would like them to be. A positive attitude is good for your health. Having a positive attitude is likely to result in more positive results and outcomes in your life. It's also more likely to lead to success, prosperity and happiness than would having a negative attitude.

15

Getting what we want in life depends more on *attitude* than on our looks, family background, education/degree, skills, knowledge or people we know. Although these things may be the first things people observe and know about us, our attitude is likely to be the first thing people use to judge *who we are*. Our attitude has a major influence on our thoughts, feelings, behavior, decisions and how we deal with things that happen to us in life. Some claim that 85%–90% of what we get in life is the direct result of our attitude.

16

What others say about us is what *they* think of or want to believe about us. It's based on how they have interpreted what they have heard or observed about us. Or it may be based on jealously, hate or a need to validate themselves. It's merely what they think or want to believe, and it isn't necessarily true. Learn to ignore the negative things people say about you but do listen to what they say. Hearing what others say about us provides us with an opportunity to take an objective look at ourselves so that we can *improve* ourselves if what they have said is true. If what they say isn't true, simply let it go.

17

Your reputation is one of the most important things about you. It's what other people *know* about you. It's the belief others have of how you are (for instance, honest or dishonest, polite or impolite, modest or arrogant). It follows you wherever you go. It tells people what to expect when they meet or deal with you. It takes time; months, even years, to build a *good* reputation but it can be destroyed in days, even in minutes or in seconds. Once it's destroyed, it might never be regained. Build a good reputation and protect the reputation you have built.

18

To be happy in life, we need to be true to ourselves. This means living our life based on our core values. These values are what's essential or important to us in ourselves (and in others) as a person. For instance, honesty and loyalty. They guide us in how to be and how to live our life. They determine whether we are or aren't comfortable with what we or other people do. Take the time to determine and think about your core values. Adjust or delete those that aren't right for you and add new ones that are.

19

No one likes an arrogant or narcissistic person. Be proud but modest. Being proud but modest means feeling good about what we can do and what we have done but not bragging to others about those things. Bragging begins when we tell people what we can do or have done with the aim to influence how they think of us. Pride is good. It can generate confidence. Confidence leads to an *I can do* mindset. This leads to achieving more in life and to a better you. Don't underestimate or undersell or overestimate or oversell yourself. Find the right balance.

20

He who asks is a fool for five minutes, but he who does not ask remains a fool forever.[3] Ask questions and get answers. Don't trust just anyone for an answer. Don't ask a friend unless you are looking for an opinion or you know for certain that your friend has an objective, factual answer. Ask someone who truly knows. It may be worse to ask someone who really doesn't know than to not ask at all. If the answers you seek are important, don't merely ask one person, ask a few people who know or should know the answers (such as a professional).

21

Know how to listen, and you will profit even from those who talk badly.[4] Truly listen to what people are saying. This means hearing what is actually being said, not what we want to hear. To do so, we need to stay objective so that our emotions, biases, opinions and perception don't influence or distort what is or has been said. Truly listening enables us to better *understand* people; who they are and what they want to say. Listening can also enable us to hear things (good or bad) that may help us to improve ourselves and to get more of what we want in life.

22

If you continue doing what you have always done or how you have always done it, you are likely to get what you have always gotten. If you're stuck in a rut or you aren't happy with what you're getting or where you're heading in your life, it may be time to do things *differently*. You may need to change what you think or believe. You might need to learn something new that will enable you to do things a different way. If you want things to change, you must be comfortable with change. You must also know how to change and when to do things differently.

23

To be truly happy in life, you need to be happy with who you are. *Do not let it be your aim to be something, aim to be someone.*[5] To be something means to do or become successful at something, such as being a teacher, singer or surgeon. To be *someone* means to be, for instance, a respectful, sincere, honest, kind, polite and compassionate human being. Accept the things about yourself that you can't change (e.g., height), change the things you can change (e.g., attitude, values and manners), and aim to become the best person you can be.

24

To be yourself in a world that is constantly trying to make you something else is the greatest accomplishment.[6] Pretty much everything on TV, radio, the Internet and in print media aims to influence us to: do, buy, think, believe or feel something. To be who you wish to be and to live how you wish to live life, you need to recognize *when and how* others are trying to influence you. Once you do, you can prevent it from making you something or someone you aren't or don't desire to be or doing something you don't want to do.

25

How you say something is as important as what you say. Be polite, confident and respectful and speak to the person not at them. Smile and look people in the eye when you talk to them. Say what you mean and mean what you say. Maintain control of your emotions. When you mean Yes – confidently say *Yes*. When you mean No – respectfully say *No*. When you say No, No is all you need to say. No explanation needed if you don't want to explain nor do you need to say you're sorry that you said No if you're not.

26

Honesty makes life simpler and easier. Say it how it really is but be tactful and sensitive. A lie can lead to stress; worrying about slipping up and having to explain ourselves to those we were dishonest with. Being caught lying can result in looking like a fool or others distrusting what we say. Both are sure to damage our reputation and we may end up losing our friends. As for *white lies*, we all tell them but they're still lies. We can be honest and also avoid hurt feelings by being creative in the way we word what we say. For instance, if given a gift we don't like, *thanks for thinking of me* rather than *it's just what I wanted*.

27

You need to love yourself. When we love ourselves, we will want the best for ourselves. We will take control of our life and control where we are going in life. We will want to fix, change and improve things that we wish or need to fix, change or improve in ourselves and in our life. When we love ourselves, we can happily be by ourselves when we feel like being by ourselves. We won't need others to be happy, but being with others will make us happy. All of this can lead to a better, healthier and happier life.

28

Now is the time to become the person you really want to be. Don't wait for *someday*. Start today. Decide who you want to be. Think about what you truly think, believe and value. Think about how you feel about things. Discover your character strengths and weaknesses. Know what you are passionate about and what makes you truly happy. Check your attitude, whether it's positive or negative. Acknowledge any masks that you wear. Identify what is and has been stopping you from being who you want to be. Then fix, improve, change, add or eliminate whatever needs to be to become who you wish to be.

PART 2
Health

Without health life is not life.

Buddha

29

A key to a long and healthy life is to exercise throughout your whole life. Aim for at least 30 minutes of moderate or 15 minutes of intense physical exercise 5 to 6 days a week.[7] Find an activity (or two) that you enjoy doing to get exercise and do it at or near your home. By doing so, you're more likely to exercise, even on days you might not feel like exercising. Do it in the morning, if possible, so that you don't skip it at the end of the day when you're likely to be tired from your day.*

30

If you stop exercising, the longer it's been since you stopped the more difficult it will be to start it again. If you're currently doing and enjoying a physical activity, be it the gym, dance, tennis, whatever it may be, don't allow your life to get so busy that you stop doing it. If it's good for your health, make time to do it. Regular exercise improves your overall health. This includes your self-esteem and self-confidence. A healthy level of both makes you happier and can enable you to achieve more and get more in life.

* Talk with your doctor before starting an exercise program.

31

Include moderate-intensity *cardiovascular exercise* into your day. Cardiovascular exercises are those activities that increase your heart rate for a period of time. Cycling, brisk walking or taking the stairs rather than the elevator are cardiovascular activities that you could do on your way to and back from work or shopping. Dancing or doing jumping jacks are things you can do when at home. Cardiovascular exercises are good for things like strengthening our heart and muscles, improving our brain power during the day and helping us to sleep better at night.

32

Include resistance training at least twice a week for all major muscle groups as part of your exercise routine.[8] Resistance training is muscle-strengthening weight bearing exercises, such as weight lifting using free weights or machines or exercises that use your body's own resistance. Also include stretching and balance exercises in your exercise routine. 10 to 15 minutes everyday helps to keep the muscles flexible, strong, and healthy. You might consider Yoga or tai chi, which can be done in a group or alone at home.

33

Walking is one of the best exercises you can do. Not only is walking good for our muscles, it can strengthen our heart, boost our immune system, improve blood circulation and burn excess calories, which helps us to lose weight or maintain a healthy weight. It may also reduce the risk of diabetes and some cancers. Walking is also good for our mental health. It could help to reduce the risk of dementia and Alzheimer's disease as we get older. Walk more. It's free and requires no equipment.

34

Regular exercise relieves stress and anxiety and improves our mood. It can increase our energy level and lead to better sleep. It can promote a better sex life. It can help protect our skin and delay signs of aging. It may also increase our chances of living longer. You simply feel better if you exercise on a regular basis. This can enable you to have more fun in life. Healthy people look healthy. Looking healthy attracts other healthy people. Being around healthy people can often lead us to live a healthier life style, eating better and exercising more.

35

Sex can be a great form of mild to moderate exercise. During sex, our legs, abdominal, chest, back, shoulders, arms and butt muscles can get a good workout. The more creative we are with our body when having sex, the more muscles our body uses and thus a better workout. Sex can also be a good form of stretching. However, to qualify as exercise, sex should involve at least 15 minutes of sweat producing activity. That's good news. The bad new is, quickies aren't going to replace your primary form of exercise.

36

You are what you eat. It's your body, your health. Take full responsibility for it. Eat healthy food. Healthy food has a positive effect on our body, inside and out. This includes our heart, lungs, brain, bones, liver, muscles, skin, teeth, hair and our mental and emotional well-being. Healthy food provides us with the energy to perform better at work, play and in bed. Eating healthy food gives us a much better chance of living a *long, happy and healthy life*. Read food and drink labels and know what you're putting into your body before you do.

37

When healthy, a regular visit to the doctor can help to find any non-symptomatic health issues early. If found early, things can often be dealt with before they destroy your health. When you don't feel right, visit your doctor as soon as you can and tell him or her all that you know, even the embarrassing things. Your doctor can't help if he or she doesn't know all the facts. (Realize that doctors do make mistakes (we all do) and can misdiagnose. If advised to take strong medication or to have surgery, get a second opinion. It's your body.)

38

Maintaining a healthy weight will make your life better. Being overweight increases your risk of a number of physical health issues. It can also lead to social, mental and emotional issues, such as, depression and loneliness, low self-esteem and being subject of ridicule, humiliation and discrimination. Being underweight can also lead to various physical, social, mental and emotional issues and consequences. A BMI (Body Mass Index) of 19 to 25 is considered to be healthy. Find out your BMI, talk with a doctor and do what you need to do to fit and stay within that range.

39

Take good care of your teeth. A good set of white choppers (teeth) is great for your self-esteem. With a good set of teeth, you are more likely to smile more. This will attract people you want to be attracted to you. Your teeth may even get you a better job. If your teeth are crooked, get them straightened. If your teeth are stained or discolored, look into getting them whitened. And avoid or limit foods, drinks and activities (such as coffee, smoking and some high-impact sports) that could have a negative effect on your teeth.

40

Getting a good night's sleep is essential for our physical, emotional, psychological, social, even financial well-being. Aim to get seven to nine hours of quality (restful and restorative) sleep every night. A good night's sleep has a positive affect on how we think, feel and act. It can increase our productivity throughout the day, improve our decision making and can even save our life. To sleep better, don't bring your problems and worries into the bedroom. Keep your bedroom clean, peaceful, stress-free and simple (uncluttered) and use it only for sleep (and sex).

41

You need to exercise your brain. As with physical exercise, *brain exercise is essential* for a healthy brain. Brain exercises can improve our memory, focus and concentration. They can improve our social skills and can also help to lower the risk of mental disease later in life. You can exercise your brain by learning something new each day. Playing games in a book of brain games, even brushing your teeth with your non-dominant hand can exercise your brain. Keep in mind, if you don't use it, one day you may lose it.

42

Healthy habits lead to a better life. These are activities and behavior that benefit our physical, emotional and mental well-being. This includes things like, having breakfast, drinking enough water during the day, eating right the rest of the day, some form of exercise every day, time outside and spending *quality time* with friends. Bad (unhealthy) habits, on the other hand, such as, donuts for breakfast or no breakfast, junk food during the day, lying on the sofa most of the day and spending too much time on the computer with virtual friends, lead to a disappointing life.

43

Recognizing your feelings and knowing what triggered those feelings will give you better control of your life. Our feelings affect our thinking and behavior. Our thinking and behavior effects our health and life. For instance, if we are angry, we may make a bad decision or lash out at someone. We might use drugs or alcohol to *temporarily* deal with that anger. Recognizing our feelings and what triggered them can enable us to deal with them rationally *before* they have a negative effect on our health or life.

44

Drugs and alcohol are not going to make you happier, sexier or more appealing. In fact, drugs and alcohol are likely to have the opposite effect, especially if abused. They are likely to lead to physical, mental, emotional, financial and social problems. They can really mess up your life and could even kill you. Drugs and alcohol are often used to hide, forget about or escape from problems or issues in life that need to be dealt with. It's your health and life. Deal with your problems and issues. Drugs and alcohol won't make them go away. Get help if you need help.

45

Smoking doesn't make you look sexy or cool. In fact, knowing what we know about the harmful effects of smoking, smoking makes you look stupid. In addition to having *ashtray mouth*, yellowing teeth and your hair and clothes smelling like what you are smoking, smoking can harm almost every part of your body, inside and out. Smoking also costs you money, can turn people off and they may avoid you, can lead to premature aging of the face and it's likely to shorten your life. If you smoke now, it's never too late to stop. Stop for your health and those you love.

46

Spending time outside is good for you. Being outside often leads to exercising, even if simply moving your body and walking. It has a positive effect on our heart, immune system and on our mental health. The sun provides vitamin D, which is *necessary* for maintaining healthy bones. But when outside, keep in mind that too much time in the sun can lead to dehydration, exhaustion and damage to your hair. It can also lead to wrinkles, brown spots, leather like skin and skin cancer. When out, hydrate and use sunscreen.

47

Stress can mess with your health. Stress can be triggered by things like: something not right at school, work or in a relationship; social media and social comparisons; lack of money and uncertainty of the future. Stress can lead to high blood pressure and heart disease. It can lead to drug and alcohol abuse. It could even kill you. Recognize when you are stressed and the cause behind it and deal with it before it screws you up. If you are unable to manage stress on your own, get help.

48

Guys – regularly check your balls for lumps or anything that feels abnormal. If you detect anything, see your doctor. Self examinations *can help to identify* testicular cancer early. If you feel weird about doing it, man up. If not man enough, ask your girlfriend or lover to do it for you.

Girls – regularly check your breasts for lumps or anything that feels abnormal. Additionally, see your doctor on a regular basis for other female body parts examinations. Such examinations can help to identify cancer early. Early detection can save your life.[9]

PART 3
Work Money Success

The key to success is action, and the essential in action is perseverance.

Sun Yat-sen

49

Choose a job you love, and you will never have to work a day in your life.[10] Work takes up about 8 to 12 hours of our day 5 days a week. That's 2000 – 3000 hours a year. Then there's the time it takes to get ready for, to get to and get back from and to unwind after work. That another 500 – 1500 hours a year of your life. Your job could easily take up to 3500 hours of your year. That's about 150 days a year working 24 hours each of those days. Wouldn't it be much nicer if those 3500 hours were spent doing what you love doing?

50

Interest, enjoyment and satisfaction in what you do to earn an income is far more important than the money. You will be spending a lot of your life working so find a career or profession that requires you to do things that interest you, that you enjoy and get satisfaction from doing. When considering a career or profession, ask yourself – is money (the income) or prestige one of the main reasons why you want that type of job or to work in that field? If it is, it's probably wise to talk with someone who is doing or has done that type of work to find out if it will truly be interesting, enjoyable and satisfying *for you*.

51

Chances are you will change jobs or career more than once in your life. In fact, doing so can often make life so much more interesting and rewarding. Rather than anticipate it, plan it. You might make it part of your life plan to, for instance, study to become a paralegal and then work in a law firm for 5-10 years. Then study to be a medical technician and work in a hospital or clinic for the next 5-10 years. And then maybe you become a teacher or a writer to share what you've learned over those years.

52

The more you know, the more money you can make/earn. Take the time to learn more and to improve skills you already have. This can enable you to charge people more for your skills and time. This could get you *more money* or give you *more time* (as you work less to earn what you earned before). To learn more, you could take classes online that are relevant to what you do. Some are free and some offer a certificate upon completion of the class. You could also work for someone (even for free) during your free time who has the skills you need or wish to improve.

53

Work smart, not hard. Use your brain not your body. Save your body energy for exercise and fun. Things that can help us to work smart include: good time management skills, thinking outside the box (creativity) to create ways to accomplish a task in the most efficient way using the least amount of time and energy, and following the 80/20 rule (if it can be applied). (The 80/20 rule purposes that roughly 80% of results often come from 20% of input (effort/activity performed). The aim is to identify the 20% and focus on that.)

54

Minimum wage sucks. If you don't have a solid plan in place that will enable you to earn a good income, learn a trade, go to trade-school, *as soon as you can*. (Learn to be a computer technician, plumber, paralegal, etc.) Many courses *only take* a year or two to complete. Having a trade can greatly improve your chances of not ending up stuck for life working for minimum wage (in an unskilled low paying job). There will always be a demand for qualified tradespeople, paying far more than minimum wage. Even if you do have a solid plan in place, having a trade is great to fall back on if that plan doesn't work out.

55

Never pay full price for anything. If you do, you are paying too much. Learn how to negotiate. When you think it's a good price, negotiate a little more. Online is a great place to find good prices. There are always bargains; Black Friday and Cyber Monday sales, first-time customer offers, coupons and sites selling overstocks at reduced prices. When you do buy, use cash-back and reward credit cards (*pay the card off in full the following month!*). But always remember, time is money. The time you spend searching or negotiating might not be worth the money saved.

56

You must save money. Set a budget and have financial goals. Avoid debt and pay off debt as soon as possible (Interest on debt can kill you financially.) Spend less than you earn and save or invest the rest. Look at investment options available to you. Learn about those that interest you and invest wisely. Pay yourself first by putting at least 5–10% of your income into investments and *appreciating* assets. When your income increases, don't spend all of that increase (unless that money is to be used to enable you to make and save more money).

57

The price of something is what we pay but what is more important is the *value* of what we pay for. The value of something (goods, services or experiences) is subjective. In other words, the value of something is its importance or usefulness for the person who wants, needs or has it. For instance, in a rational world, the value of a pair of old shoes for a person who has no shoes would be much higher than the value for a person who has many pairs of shoes.

58

Buying anything *on impulse* is almost always the wrong thing to buy. Mass media advertising and "infomercials" and supermarket managers are masters at getting us to buy stuff we don't really need. Many of these things soon find themselves forgotten in a kitchen cupboard, in a closet or in a box in the garage. Buying on impulse is sure to have a negative effect on your budgeting and financial goals. Save your money, be smart and more rational the next time you're about to buy something on impulse. Know what motivates impulse buying and say NO to things that you don't really need or won't use.

59

Less often means more. Buying less stuff can often mean more money, time, energy, freedom and experiences. In addition to money, the cost to buy something is the time and energy spent to earn the money to buy it. It's also the cost of not having or not doing something else that you could have spent the money, time or energy on. Think before you buy. If it's for you, ask yourself – do I really need this? Is it something that will be useful or help to make my life easier or better? If you don't or it won't, it is probably a good decision to not buy it.

60

A man in debt is so far a slave.[11] Debt can have a negative effect on your life. It can destroy your health and relationships. It can also take away your freedom. If you are in debt, getting out of debt should be a top priority. Have a plan and follow it. Credit cards (to be paid off *in full* when due) are for convenience, not to pay for things you don't have money to pay for. Loans (to be paid off as *quickly* as possible) should only be to pay for things that appreciate (e.g., land, houses, condos, and maybe, to start your own business).

61

Real estate is one of the best investments. Buy a condo or a house as soon as you can – and pay off the loan as quickly as possible. If you can't afford to live in it yourself, rent it out. The rent will help you to pay off the loan. The *right* real estate can be a great long-term investment as the value is likely to increase over time. It can also eventually generate *passive income*. Owing a condo or house without a mortgage is one of the most valuable things to have when you are older. (Along with health and good friends.)

62

Think twice before you buy. Always remember when you shop, nothing is a bargain if you don't really need it. There are always *bargains – special* prices at supermarkets, department and home improvement stores, and online. There will always be things offered at a discount that may appeal to you that you likely don't really need. Take a list when you go to the supermarket and stick to that list. Refrain from window shopping at brick and mortar stores. And be careful when browsing online shopping websites. Guaranteed there will be something you'll convince yourself you need to buy that you really don't need.

63

Becoming rich is a mindset. Those who *believe* that they cannot or will not be rich, are likely to not be rich. Those who believe they can or will, probably will. To become rich requires thinking about and doing the things needed to become and stay rich. It's about saving, investing and looking for, and importantly creating, opportunities and *acting on* those opportunities. The rich are rich because they focus on building things, like businesses, and accumulating assets that are likely to increase in value over time (such as real estate, blue chip stocks and learning).

64

Our greatest weakness lies in giving up. The most certain way to succeed is always to try just one more time.[12] For most of us, becoming successful is a long term project. It requires being patient and putting off immediate or short term gratification for long term gain. It means pushing ourselves and not stopping until we get what we want – to be successful. It requires the mental and emotional ability to recover from set-backs and finding different ways to do things if what we did the first time didn't get us what we wanted.

65

The price of anything is the amount of life you exchange for it.[13] Our time is our life. When we work, we exchange our time (part of our life) for money (our pay). Each hour we work to earn money is an hour of our life. If we make $15 an hour and we buy a hat for $120, the hat cost (we exchanged) eight hours of our life (working) to buy it. Same applies to doing something. If we watch TV for an hour, the price to do so is an hour of our life. The older we get the less life we have to exchange. Exchange it wisely.

66

To create wealth and to enjoy it, you need to be healthy. Those with poor health tend to lack energy, creativity, productivity and a positive attitude, all of which are needed to earn, create and hold onto wealth. Those in poor health are also likely to need to spend their time (and money) dealing with their poor health, time which could be used to create and enjoy their wealth. Don't allow yourself to be so busy in life earning or creating wealth that your health suffers. Make the time everyday to take care of your health. If you lose it, it may be gone forever. Once it's gone, wealth can't buy you good health.

67

Increasing your earning potential (being paid the most possible for your time) is one of the best investments you can make. Charging more for your time (life) can give you more time (life). To increase you earning potential, you need to learn more and improve your skills. This might mean learning to do what you do better, quicker or cheaper. Or it could mean specializing in what you do, being an expert in the things you do. Working a second job to earn more money is counter-productive (*exchanging more* of your life). Use that time to *increase* the $ value of your time.

68

By desiring little, a poor man makes himself rich.[14]
Beyond the basic needs we all require to live life comfortably (food, shelter, clean air and water, health, love, friends, safety and variety (adventure, challenge, change), we don't need much to be rich. To be rich means to be in control of our life. Control means *freedom*, freedom to be whom and do, say and think what we desire. It means being financially (having *enough* money to live) and emotionally independent. It also means time to do what we need and want to do. Too much desire can take that freedom away.

69

The lack of (or lust for) money is the root of all evil.[15] Not having *enough* money (or desiring too much money) can lead to lying, cheating, stealing and doing things that we would probably rather not do. *Enough* is subjective. You need to determine how much is enough for you, for now and in the future. There are numerous formulas out there. To get you started, think about how much you would need to be able to be in control of your life (see 68). Also keep in mind that it *isn't really about money*, but rather about income – the best of which is passive income. (See 71)

70

No matter how many people or how often people tell you that money isn't important, they're wrong. Used wisely, money can lead to a much better life for you, for those you care about, and even for those you don't even know (by giving to charities). It's unlikely that you will make a lot of money on a salary or hourly wage alone. You need to start learning, earning, making and creating money today. Read about how rich people have made their money and put into action things that will work for you. And make or create things that will earn you more money.

71

The easiest way to financial independence (and making a lot of money) is *passive income*. This is income from things such as: intellectual property, rental property, websites and affiliate marketing. All enable you to earn money 24/7. Intellectual property (a book, music, computer program, cell phone app or game, an invention, etc.) is one of the best passive income sources. It can earn royalties (sometimes providing an income for life) and is often taxed at a lower rate than income from working a job. *Intellectual property – work once, get paid forever*. Start creating today.

72

That some achieve great success is proof to all that others can achieve it as well.[16] Successful people have the exact same number of hours in a day that we have. The difference is, they know how to manage their time. They use their time more efficiently and on things that will help them to get what they want in life. (Study rather than watching TV, for instance.) Being successful is not luck. It's knowing what you want, using time wisely, finding and creating opportunities, being creative, and doing what needs to be done to get what you want.

73

The mind is everything. What you think you become.[17] The things we think about and focus on during the day influence who we are, who we can become, what we do and what we get in life. This includes becoming and being successful. Before you can succeed, first you need to know what success is. Success is (should be) subjective. That is, being successful should be what YOU define it to be, not what other people say it is or claim it to be. Once you know what success is for you, you can start thinking and focusing on that.

74

Success (for me) is being your true self and doing things you want to do. This means not being like others or doing things everyone else is doing if that isn't who you want to be or what you want to do. It's doing things that you like doing that are: purposeful, good for your overall well-being and that bring you joy and happiness. It's moving forward by having a purpose in life and achieving it. It's being an honest, giving and caring person. It's also knowing that you did your best at whatever you do. The more often you do the things in *your* definition of success, the more successful you are.

75

Life changes. Chances are, what you want to do in life and where you want to do it will change. This is likely to include your job or career. To be prepared for change, gain knowledge and develop a set of flexible skills that can enable you to get a job in various occupations and locations. Flexibility enables us to adapt to changes so that we can earn an income even if our life or what we have been doing to earn or create an income changes along the way. Things like: negotiation skills, computer software skills and a foreign language or two could help prepare you for change.

76

You can't have it all. It's not possible to success with all of your goals and satisfy all your desires. To be successful at something requires making sacrifices in other areas of our life. Time spent to achieve success in one thing will be less time available to do other things. The aim is to create the *right balance*. To do this, we need to set time limits (time spent) on the things we wish to do and be successful doing or reduce the things we wish to do or aim to succeed at. Otherwise, we can miss out on other important things in life.

PART 4
Relationships

One of the most beautiful qualities of a great relationship is to understand and to be understood.

Lucius Annaeus Seneca

77

The most important relationship in our life is the one we have with ourselves. When we like ourselves, we value ourselves. When we value ourselves, we'll take the time and make the effort to take care of our physical, mental, emotional and social health and well-being. We'll be more positive and much more likely to make choices and decisions that are right for us. We won't allow anyone to mistreat us and we'll stop wasting our time trying to please other people. All of this will make our life happier.

78

We can change things in ourselves and in our life but we can't change other people. People change only when *they* believe that they need to change, they want to change and they take action to change. Pushing or nagging someone to change isn't going to change that person. However, it may change (have a negative effect on) the relationship with that person. Rather than spend your time trying to change others, spend the time discovering and changing things that need change in yourself and in your life. This may lead to a positive change in the relationship with the person you think needs to change.

79

The only way to have a friend is to be one.[18] Being a true friend shows the person that you are friends with what you're happy to give as a friend and what you expect in a friend. True friends have a positive impact on our health and life. They can increase our sense of belonging and thus our feeling of self-worth (value). They can help us to get through the difficult times in our life and encourage us to follow our dreams. Being and having true friends brings more happiness into our friends' lives and ours.

80

Being connected with people may be the second most important (health being first) and necessary element for a happy and healthy life. We are social creatures, our brain is wired to be connected with other people. To get the benefits of this connection requires face-to-face interaction, truly listening and having the patience to truly understand. It requires time, being honest with that person and being *genuinely concerned* about their well-being. And it requires being there and helping that person whenever you can. Take the time and make the effort to stay truly connected with your family and true friends.

81

When it comes to friends, *quality is infinitely more important* than quantity. Choose your friends wisely. The people you choose to share your life with will make all the difference in your life. Choose people who are positive, who respect you, listen to you and who sincerely care about you. Choose people who share many of your beliefs and values and who have similar standards, likes and dislikes. And choose those who will support your dreams and goals, and importantly who want you to be you.

82

Don't judge a book (person) by its cover. Outer appearances can hide inner flaws and can also conceal strengths and true beauty. Most people aren't who they may appear to be on the outside. Some are hiding behind masks to pretend to be who they aren't. Others may be shy or unapproachable so to hide insecurities. How people dress, look, talk, walk or act isn't necessarily an indication of who they really are. Nor does fame or fortune say much about who a person really is. Take the time to find out who a person you wish to know really is, who they are on the inside, and don't judge those you haven't.

83

When spending time with friends, make it *quality time*. Quality time means truly being there, giving your friend or friends your full attention. It means being enthusiastic about and actively participating in whatever you are doing when with your friend. It means truly listening to what they are saying and looking at them when you are talking to them and they are talking to you. It also means no texting, web-browsing, calling, or holding onto your phone waiting for someone to call you. Be a real friend. Put your phone away when with a friend, better yet, turn it off.

84

You don't have to do something for someone you don't want to and really don't need to do. Be honest and polite and simply say *No*. Don't say, *I'll think about it* or *maybe later* if you don't want to and don't need to do it. Don't feel obligated or feel guilty. No need to be sorry or say sorry if you don't want to do it. Just tell the person that you can't, don't want to or don't have the time. Saying *No* will give you more time and energy to focus on and do other things you want or need to do for others and for yourself.

85

If you want something done how and when you want it done, *do it yourself*. If you ask someone to do something for you (and you aren't paying them to do it), let them do it their way. Don't tell them how to do it or push them to do it when they aren't ready to do it. By letting them do it their way and when they want to do it, they're more likely to be happier to do things for you in the future. But if you tell them how and when to do it when they aren't ready to do it, chances are they will learn how to say *No*.

86

Life is easier if you keep your nose out of other people's personal business. This includes your best friend's personal business (unless he or she clearly asks for your comments or help). At the same time, don't let people stick their nose into your personal business, if you don't want them to. If someone asks you something you do not want to share (they stick their nose into your business), don't share it. Don't get angry. Don't play games. Simply and politely tell the person straight out that you don't wish to share it – *It's private*. If they persist, walk away.

87

The people we spend time with influence what we think and believe, how we feel and what we do. These things will determine who we become, what we get and where we go in life. For instance, if you hang out with losers, you're very likely to become one too. If you hang out with winners, chances are you will *be a winner*. Spend your time with positive, happy, fun and productive people. Spend time with people who inspire you, who know more than you and who have higher standards than you so that you can grow.

88

Guys – respect the girls you date (and marry). This means being polite and watching your language. It means making eye contact when talking to her, letting her talk, genuinely listening to her, asking for her opinion and accepting that her opinion is as valid as your own. It also means being well-groomed (face/hair/hands clean and tidy), smelling good and dressing appropriately for the event or occasion And don't forget to observe her body language so to ensure that she's OK with you touching her body, before you do (and when you do, doing so gradually so to give her time to know what you're up to).

89

Girls – respect yourself when you date (and get married). This means to be yourself. It means not pretending to be the girl you think he wants you to be. This includes doing things you would not normally do, like getting drunk or stoned, because that's what you think he wants you to do. It means *not* putting yourself down or dumbing-down if you happen to be smarter than he is. It also means saying what you want or need to say, saying *No* when you feel and mean No and walking away if any guy treats you badly.

90

Successful relationships require a lot, such as:

- *effective* communication – able to exchange information and to express thoughts, feelings, ideas, expectations, wants and needs with each other
- willingness to work on difficulties together
- compromise – able to find *common ground* (give and take) between each other in order to reach agreement to move forward
- complete loyalty to, trust in and honesty with each other, and
- ability to forgive (most things).

91

Successful relationships also require:

- respect for privacy and space – being fine with each other spending time with their friends even if they aren't your friends
- compassion and empathy and the ability to provide emotional support to each other
- quality time together
- humor, laughter and having fun together
- consistent appreciation of each other, and
- having and planning for the future of that relationship together.

92

Sex (is) should be fun for those having sex. Know what you like when having sex and don't accept anything less. Sex and intimacy impacts every aspect of our life, including our physical, emotional, mental, social and even intellectual health.* Sex enables us to connect with people (physically, mentally and emotionally). Having good (intimate) sex with someone can release endorphins in the brain, which can help to relieve anxiety and stress. Sex is good for us and fun sex can add to our overall happiness.

* American Sexual Health Association

93

Recognize and accept that in any personal relationship: true friendship, marriage or living with someone, life consists of:

1. your life
2. the other person's life, and
3. a joint life (what you and the other person do together).

Both you and the other person need to be truly committed to and respect those lives and allow each other time, without resentment, resistance, unhealthy jealously or pressure, to live life.

94

Before you decide to live with someone as a couple, find out as much as you can about that person before you do. For instance, do they respect you. Are they mature enough for a serious relationship. Are their values similar to yours and do they have similar likes, dislikes and interests. Do they flirt a lot or are they known to cheat on their partners. Are they overly jealous. Are they a slob or hoarder? Are they abusive or do they abuse drugs or alcohol. Do they lie or steal. Are they truly compatible and a good communicator. And also, do they know who you really are.

95

Choose your future husband/wife/partner very carefully. This one decision is very likely to determine whether you will or won't be happy in life. People are different. Some differences may be hidden deep inside, which may reveal themselves months or years later. If you don't have a pretty good idea of who that person is, chances are those difference may have a significant negative effect on your happiness. And remember, if you choose someone with the hope that they will change into someone who you really want to be with, chances are, they won't.

96

There is no perfect marriage. In fact, on average, 40-50% of marriages end up in divorce. A good marriage depends on *two things*: finding the right person for you and you being the right person for them. Decide what you are looking for in a partner and know whether that person can provide you with what you need and want. Also discover (ask) what that person needs and wants and ask yourself if you are able and willing to provide it. A good marriage depends on making the right choice. Let your brain do the choosing.

97

Know what you're getting into before you get into it. If you are thinking of getting into a relationship or getting married (especially if that person has been married before), before you do – check for and into any and all undesirable *baggage* that comes with that person. This can include things like: a jealous ex-boyfriend, girlfriend or spouse, odd ex-in laws, kids with issues or kids you don't know about, drugs or alcohol abuse, debt or past or present legal issues.

98

Love can fade, so too can good looks. A lumpy butt, big belly or a winkled face is sure to put a quick end to a marriage/live-together relationship based on good looks. Choose your partner based on compatibility and ability to communicate with each other. (Looks are a bonus.) Both lead to companionship; enjoying spending time with each other. *True companionship* will unlikely fade. Being with someone who isn't compatible, says nothing or has nothing to say, or talks about stuff you have little or no interest in is sure to lead to an *unhappy* and *unhealthy* relationship.

99

Never take advantage of someone in a relationship. Taking advantage includes: lying, cheating, being unfair and manipulating the other person to do or not do something. Be trustworthy, respectful, compromising, honest and grateful. If someone is kind to you, let them know that you appreciate their kindness. When you appreciate someone, tell them that you do. When you love someone, be sure to show them that you love them. Doing so is good for you, and chances are it will make them feel good too.

100

The quality of your relationships is far more important than the number of people you know or call your friend. Having a lot of acquaintances and unnecessary or second-rate relationships can make life busier and more complicated. People who have a *circle of a few true friends* tend to: be less stressed, have better emotional and mental health, have happier lives and live longer than those who don't. They are inclined to have a higher level of self-esteem, and therefore they are likely to feel less nervous or awkward when with people they don't know. This makes it easier for them to meet and deal with other people.

PART 5
Happiness

Those who enjoy doing and enjoy what they have done are happy.

Johann Wolfgang von Goethe

Happiness

101

Happiness isn't what other people may say or try to convince us it is. It's not something that we can buy in the store or online. It's not something we can find in drugs or alcohol. Happiness is something that we need to *create* for and from within ourselves. Happiness is *feeling good about ourselves*, experiencing positive emotions, having a sense of meaning and purpose in life and being satisfied and content with the direction we are going in life. It's what we feel, think and experience. All of this arises from within.

102

When you look back on your life, you're sure to regret the things you didn't do more than the things you didn't buy. Happiness is found in enjoying doing the things we do in life (*experiencing life*) and having enjoyed the things that we have done. Happiness is not found in material things. *Material things* are merely physical objects that people try to convince us we need to have (buy) to be happy. The more things we buy (more time spent working to make money to buy), the less time we have to do things we enjoy doing. If you *believe* that material things make you happy, chances are you'll miss out on being happy.

103

Happiness depends upon ourselves.[19] To be happy, we need to make it happen. We need to be who we wish to be doing what we want to do in life. We need challenges and variety. We need to try new things to find more things that we enjoy doing. We need to put ourselves in places and situations that will enable us to be who we wish to be doing things we want to do with people we want to do those things with. We also need to avoid places, situations and people that interfere with or prevent us from being happy.

104

When we are happy with who we are on the inside, there is little that we need to find outside ourselves to be happy. The more content we are with ourselves (as a person) and with our non-material life (conditions/environment), the *fewer* material things we will want or need. This will give us more time (and money) to improve ourselves and the conditions and environment we live in. It might be improving our self-confidence so that we can set higher goals to achieve. Or it may be to learn more to earn more so that we can afford to live in a better neighborhood. Small improvements lead to *big increases* in happiness.

105

Being in control of who we are and what we do in life leads to happiness. Control enables us to think and believe what we wish to think and believe. It enables us to feel how we instinctively feel. It enables us to make our own choices and decisions and to set and achieve goals that we wish to achieve. This enables us to do what we want and need to do to be happy in life. If you allow people, relationships, your job or career or the media to control or manipulate you, you are giving them the power to control your happiness.

106

Expect nothing from anyone (other than yourself). By doing so, you won't be disappointed when they don't do or say as you expected. People often do and say what they think or believe is the right thing to do or say. When they do, they often fail to *take into consideration* what others may think or believe is the right thing to do or say in those circumstances. Expecting people to do, act or react a *specific way* (how you would or how you feel they should) is setting yourself up for disappointment, even resentment. This will have a negative impact on your happiness.

107

True happiness is to enjoy the present without anxious dependence upon the future.[20] Enjoy the process of doing what you're doing when you're doing it without depending on or thinking about the future outcome. If we're always depending on or thinking about the future outcome of what we're doing, we can end up missing out on enjoying the things we do. (Thinking about winning the game, missing out on enjoying playing it.) If we miss out on enjoying what we are doing in the present and the outcome we hoped for doesn't happen, we're sure to be *disappointed* (unhappy).

108

Don't expect money or fame to bring you happiness. Being rich or famous has its problems. For instance, a higher rate of income tax, little or no privacy, the cost to hire personal staff, stress, possible physical or mental health issues as a result of stress, even fake friends, stalkers or being the target for crime. Money or fame could, however, contribute to your happiness if you *use it* to: create conditions and an environment where you can be who you truly wish to be, do what you really want to do when and how you want to do it, and to help others to do the same.

109

If you want to be happy – stay healthy. What happiness means to you will change as you get older, but being and staying active (doing things) and learning and doing new things will always be a vital part of happiness. To be and stay active and to learn and do new things, we need to be healthy (physically, mentally and emotionally). Sick, weak and extremely underweight or overweight people are far more likely to be unhappy. People who are depressed, who always complain, who have low self-esteem or a negative attitude are also more likely to be unhappy.

110

Very little is needed to make a happy life; it's all within yourself, in your way of thinking.[21] Being happy is a choice, and it's our way of thinking (*our attitude*) that determines whether we choose to be happy. We need to have a positive attitude to be happy. A positive attitude can provide us with the motivation and energy we need to take positive action to do what we need to do to be happy. It also enables us to handle, deal with and overcome the unhappy things in life so that those things don't make our life unhappy. A change in attitude can increase our happiness.

111

Every morning when you wake up, you have a choice to be happy or not to be happy. *Choose to be happy.* Life is a lot better when you do. It's not difficult to be happy. The simplest things in life can bring much happiness into our life. For example, being with happy people or giving to or helping others can make our days happier. Such activities can actually produce *happy hormones* (dopamine, endorphins etc.), which can help to reduce stress and anxiety and trigger (in the brain) a feeling of happiness.

112

What we think the value of something we do will be will have an influence on our happiness. Take for instance, taking a foreign language in school. One thought might be that it's a waste of time; we'll never use it (no value not happy to have to take it) but we need to pass it to graduate (value and short term happiness for passing). Another thought might be that it's time well spent; we pass it to graduate, *learn* a foreign language, can use it to get a better job and are able to speak to locals if we choose to travel overseas (great value long lasting happiness). Same event different perceived or believed value.

113

Happiness is – financial independence. Financial independence means having enough money to live our life as we wish to live it. It means not depending on someone to support us or pay us, therefore no one controls us. It also means having more than enough money at the end of each month to save for our future financial freedom. And ideally it means that rather than having to work for money, our money is working for us – (investments) and if we choose to work, we do so not to get paid but rather to do the work we love doing and get paid to do it.

114

Happiness is – emotional independence. Emotional independence means: not needing anyone to make us happy, not feeling a need to please others, and not needing someone to boost our self-esteem or self-confidence by needing reassurance or validation from others that we are accepted or OK. It also means not equating happiness with needing to be in a relationship and not feeling a need to conform to what others tell us or want us to be. Emotional independence is about being in control of yourself and your life, being who you wish to be – happy and free.

115

A *healthy level* of self-esteem and self-confidence, feeling good about ourselves, makes us happier in life. A healthy level of self-esteem and self-confidence enables us to do more and accomplish more in life. This will make us happy. A healthy level of self-esteem and self confidence will also help us to stay healthy and will bring better friends and lovers into our life. This too is sure to make us happy. Make time to improve both your self-esteem and self-confidence, you'll be very happy that you did.

116

Don't blame other people for your problems or unhappiness. If you have a problem or things are not the way you want them to be, *you* need to find a solution or a way to deal with it. Blaming someone can stop us from taking action to fix our problems or unhappiness. If someone is the reason behind what led to your problems or unhappiness (the consequences of their action), you are the only one who can do something to fix or deal with it. That might be as simple as letting it go, letting them go or walking away. Or it may be doing or saying something or learning something new.

117

Our brain apparently has a natural *negative bias*. That is, our brain may have a stronger tendency to think of and focus on the bad and negative. This could explain why news on TV or in print media is almost always negative (news media knows this will grab our attention to watch or buy). It might also explain why so many people are unhappy. Overcoming this negative bias requires extra *conscious effort*; perhaps thinking two or more positive thoughts or doing two or more positive things to overcome one negative.

118

We experience happiness the instant we are doing or experiencing things that we enjoy. Activities that we enjoy doing but are not thinking about doing when doing them (sex or dancing, for instance) are possibly the most *instant moment experiences* possible. When our body is focused on and engrossed in what we're doing, our thoughts and what's happening around us seem to disappear. To have these instant moment experiences (bliss/happiness), find and do activities that you truly enjoy doing, don't think about doing them just allow your body to totally focus on them when doing them.

119

If you are unhappy and your life is not the way you wish it to be, look within. That's where you will find the origin of and the solution to your unhappiness. To be and remain happy, we need to accept responsibility for our life. No one else can or will. Once we have, we need to take responsibility, to take action to find solutions that will make us happy again and to enable us to make our life the way we want it to be. Blame, excuses, drugs, alcohol or climbing under a rock will not make things better or make you happy.

120

A simpler life can lead to a happier life. A simpler life means fewer choices and fewer things. Fewer choices and fewer things can reduce anxiety and stress. Having fewer choices may help us to make better decisions and spend less time choosing. The fewer material things we want or have, the more *freedom* we have. Material things require: our time working to earn money to buy those things, dusting, cleaning, repairing and sometimes insuring those things, and space in our house or garage to put those things. Less stuff = more time, money, space and happiness.

121

You are likely to be happier in life if you don't compare yourself to others. No matter how good looking or successful you are, there is and will always be someone who is better looking or more successful. No matter how much stuff you have or how much you paid for that stuff, there is and will always be someone who has more or has spent more. Comparing can lead to jealousy, stress and resentment, which is certain to make you unhappy. Rather than spend the time comparing, spend that time *improving you*.

122

We are free only insofar as we are in a position at every moment in our life to follow ourselves.[22] Happiness comes from having the choice (freedom) to make up *our own mind* and having the choice to change that choice if we choose to do so. Life is a journey, one in which we will need to choose which paths to travel. Let it be your decision which ones you choose. The choices and decisions made in your life will determine your happiness. Don't allow peer or social pressure to make them for you. Only you know (or can discover) the ones that are right for you.

123

It's a waste of time to think or worry about what other people think or say about us. Doing so can stop us from doing and saying what we want to do and say. This will have a negative effect on our happiness. The truth is, people spend most of their time thinking and talking about themselves rather than about you. When you realize this, you'll be happier. If what they do think or say is true about you, it's *your* choice and decision whether to accept those things, be happy about those things or to do something to fix or change those things in yourself. Change could help you to make your life better and happier.

124

Happiness (for me) includes:

- being fit and healthy
- free to be and do as I wish to be and do
- experiencing life
- smiling and laughing
- spending time with *real* friends
- watching kittens and puppies play
- traveling overseas
- making someone else happy

How about for you?

PART 6
Life in General

There is just one life for each of us; our own.

Euripides

125

There is nothing impossible to those who will try.[23] If we don't take action to get what we want, we simply won't get it. Whatever it may be that we wish to get, we need to try until we do. If you do not succeed the first try, *identify the why* you were unable to succeed. It might be that you lack the information or skills required to get it. Or maybe you need to find or create a different strategy or method to get what you want. But when you do acquire, find or create what you need to overcome the *why*, you need to try again.

126

Life is really simple, but we insist on making it complicated.[24] Making the wrong choices or decisions (not knowing what we need to know when we need to know it) can make life complicated. Having the wrong friends or marrying the wrong person can also make life complicated. A lack of money or having too much money often leads to a complicated life. So too does worry, stress, jealously, anger, resentment and grudges. And alcohol or drug abuse or a crappy attitude is sure to make life complicated. Know what's important in life. Let go of what isn't. Fix what needs fixing. Think. Learn to earn and choose wisely.

127

Something done often can't be undone. Something said can never be unsaid. Before doing or saying something in *reaction* to peer pressure or your emotions, take a second or two to think before you do. The wrong things done or said can mess up your life. They can lead to anger, regret, anxiety and stress, and can destroy relationships. They can clutter your mind, making it harder to think clearly and to do and say the right things. And they can consume your time and distract you from thinking about and doing other things that may get you more of what you desire in life.

128

If you don't discover what you truly want to do in and with your life, you'll miss out on living your life. Life provides us with an opportunity to create a life that's right for us. Take the time to discover what you truly want to do in and with your life – early in life. Once you have discovered what that is, do something each day that will enable you to make it all happen. Forget about aiming to live life like other people. That life is unlikely to be the life for you. Design and create your own life, one that's right for you, then live it for the rest of your life.

129

What we may think or believe (subjective) is true or real might in fact not be true or real. What is true and real is what can be verified with proof or genuine evidence that it is true or real. Once we believe something to be true or real, we tend to hang onto it, even if it isn't. It might be that we don't want to admit to ourselves that what we think or believe – isn't true or real. Or it may be that agreeing with those around us and being wrong may be safer than disagreeing and being right. Whatever it may be, knowing what is actually true and real will enable us to make better choices and decisions in and for our life.

130

We all have the same number of hours in each day. Some of us get so much accomplished in those hours. Others seem to get little done. It's how those hours are used that makes the difference. We need to use our time wisely. To use our time wisely, we need to be organized and prioritize (*do the essential and important things first* – things that will get us closer to living the life we want, things that provide us the *most benefit in return for the time spent*). We can also delegate or pay others to do things that aren't *worth our time*.

131

What you do with what happens to you (how you act or react) is more important than what happens to you.[25] When something happens to us, our brain triggers an emotional response. That emotion stimulates us to act or react. When we act, we tend to take action on what has happened. But when we react, we tend to emotionally respond to what has happened. Acting can lead to effectively dealing with what has happened. Reacting can lead to failing to deal with it or even creating more problems. For instance, a friend yells at you, you *talk it out* (act) or you *punch him* (react).

132

If you want to get things done better, *forget* about *multitasking*. Multitasking may lead to more being done but can often result in mistakes, lower quality output and less being accomplished. Apparently, our brain can only accurately perform one conscious activity at a time. This means that we (our brain) are more productive and efficient if we do one thing at a time. Try writing a text message. Simple, right. Now *try to listen* to someone talking to you at the same time – *multitask*. Feel the extra effort required to do both, to accurately text and understand what's being said?

133

The best way to prepare for the future is to take good care of the present, today. Our life today is made up of what we did and didn't do in the past. For instance, if we took care of our health in the past, chances of being healthy today are much better than if we hadn't. Today will be the past tomorrow. Our life tomorrow (the future) will be made up of what we did and didn't do in our past todays. For instance, if we invest and save today, chances of having financial freedom in the future is much greater than if we don't.

134

Our life is what our thoughts make it.[26] They determine what we do and get in our life. Our mind moves in the direction of our thoughts. If we focus on the positive, our mind will move toward the positive. That is, if we think and expect the best, chances are we will get the best. If we have positive thoughts and expectations, chances are we are more likely to take on challenges and act on opportunities, as we think and expect that we will succeed. This will get us more of what we want in life. On the other hand, if we have negative thoughts and expectations, chances are we won't. What we think is (should be) our choice.

135

Recognize what you can change and what you cannot change. Do something to change things that you can change – if they are meaningful to you or if doing so would make a positive difference in your life. (For instance, things that help you to make other people's lives better). For the things that you cannot change (things beyond your control), do what you can to limit any effect those things might have on you – then let it go. Trying to change those things is time and effort lost, both of which could have otherwise been used toward changing things you can change.

136

Believe nothing you hear and only half of what you see.[27] What people say is usually based on what they think and believe, their *subjective interpretation* of things. What we see is our *subjective interpretation* (our perception) of what we see. What society and the media tell us or show us is what they want us to hear or see. We often hear and see what we want to hear and see. And what we hear or see can be misinterpreted, inaccurate or simply not true. When what you hear or see could influence or effect what you do, know the facts before you do.

137

The secret of getting ahead is getting started.[28] If you do nothing, you get nothing. If you stand still, you are certain to go nowhere. Don't allow procrastination to slow you down or stop you from doing what you need to do to get and achieve what you want in life. Get started. Do something today. Get motivated, create an emotional connection to your future you. Visualize future benefits or rewards with doing and achieving, and pain or regret with not starting what you need to start in order to do or achieve what you need or desire in life.

138

We start to die from the day we are born. Most of us look at life as years ahead of us rather than years we have *remaining*. Don't waste your life. Do more, see more, love more, share more, experience more. If you can't do what you want to do now, do something *now* that will enable you to do it sooner rather than later. Putting things off for the distant future (aka bucket list) could mean that you might never get to do those things. Make a *To Live Life Now* list – things to do now or in the near future and do those things as soon as you can.

139

Opportunity favors those who recognize opportunities and are ready *to act on them*. Opportunities are potential paths to do what we want to do and to go where we want to go in life. They are all around us but are often not seen or are gone before we act on them. To recognize and act on opportunities, we need to know what we want and what we will need to do to get it *before* an opportunity arises. One of the major regrets in life is opportunities not acted upon. Be prepared for and act on opportunities.

140

Life is time and there is no time to waste. Most of us will have about 650,000 – 700,000 hours in our life. (A third of that is spent sleeping.) How we spend our time will make all the difference in our life. We can't buy more *life-time*. When it's gone, it's gone. Don't waste your time in bad or unless relationships or dealing with unpleasant or unreasonable people. Don't waste it arguing, complaining, giving excuses, procrastinating or worrying about the little things. And don't waste your time waiting in lines (queues), waiting for something to happen or doing things you don't enjoy doing (pay someone to do those things).

141

Timing is (almost) everything. Some might call it luck. But there is more to timing than mere luck. Timing is about a situation or activity at a particular time (when conditions are right) that if acted on can result in an optimal outcome. For us to benefit from timing, we need to recognize these situations or activities when the time and conditions are right and take appropriate action. For instance, it might be on the day you just lost your lover and your job when you hear about a teaching job in a country you've always wanted to visit – and you accept that teaching job.

142

Life is short, and it gets shorter each day. One day (*sooner than you think*) you will ask yourself where did all the years go? Don't waste your life and don't put off living. Stop telling yourself that there's still plenty of time or that you will do it *someday*. Fill your life with adventure and experiences. Travel the world, learn and do the things you have always thought about doing. Be someone special, be the best you can be, and do something special with your life. Decide who you want to be and what you want to do in and with your life and start doing it today.

143

Learn first aid. Take a course and refresher courses each year. Know how to save a life. Learn the Heimlich maneuver and cardiopulmonary resuscitation (CPR). The life you save could be a loved one. Or it might be someone you don't know who is loved by others. Saving someone's life would live inside you and the person you saved for the rest of your and their life.

144

Keep your private stuff private. Don't tell people or put on social media sites sensitive or private stuff about yourself. (This includes telling your best friend. They may not always be your friend.) Private stuff is things like how much money you have, photos of you naked or stuff you wouldn't want your mom to see you doing or know about. Once your stuff is out there, it's out there *forever* for your mom, dad, granny, friends, strangers, even prospective employers to hear or see. One exception, if you need *professional* help, you may need to reveal private stuff so that they can help. But if you do, do it in person, not on online.

145

To know the road ahead, ask those returning.[29] Learn from the experience of others. Ask those who have experienced the things you are thinking of doing (having kids is a good example) or aiming to achieve (becoming a lawyer, for instance). This could save you time, energy, money and even disappointment or pain having to experience the unexpected yourself. They likely know what to do and what not to do. They probably know the advantages, disadvantages, benefits and rewards. They may even know how to do or achieve things faster, better or more effectively.

146

Don't accept unacceptable behavior from anyone. Unacceptable behavior includes: unwanted physical contact, sexual and verbal harassment, malicious rumors or gossip, mental manipulation, intimidation and discrimination. If it happens, stay calm, tell the person(s) that their behavior is unacceptable and simply walk away. No need to explain or apologize. If they continue or can't seem to get it, it may be time to exclude them from your life; find different friends, partner, job or place to live, get legal assistance or, as a last resort, physically defend yourself. (See 7)

147

You need to do what you need to do to get what you want in life. No one is going to do it or get it for you. Know what you want. Know what you need to do to make what you want happen. Believe that you can get what you want before you set out to get it. Be prepared and aim to spend whatever time and energy it takes to do what you need to do in order to get it. Take action based on what you want, not what you expect to get. And don't listen to, believe or give power to anyone who tells you that you can't do or get what you want in life.

148

An average life is fine for those who can't do better. We can do better if we choose to do better. Don't accept life's default, merely living life. Don't live life like most people do or how society or the media has told or shown you how you are *supposed* to or are *expected* to. Instead, design, create and live a better than average life. Improve yourself. Travel the world. Do different things and do things differently. Make lifelong health and fitness and education a part of your life. Volunteer to help others (human and animal) to have a better life. Be good, do good.

149

Don't worry or be stressed about the past, it's gone. Learn from it and move forward. Focus on today. Each day is a new day to enjoy and to do new things. Don't underestimate or overestimate your future. Think about and plan for your future. Visualize yourself in the future, including at 60, 70 and 80 years old. Ask yourself what will be important when you are that age. (Health, a home and money to live, etc.) Then do something today and each day that will ensure that you will have what you will need to have.

150

Be cautious of whose advice you seek. Friends and family may have good intentions when giving advice but they might not have the right or best advice for you. Advice found on the Internet or social media sites can be wrong, bad or even dangerous. If you have a problem or issue that involves a serious matter, spend the money and get advice from a *qualified* professional. Ask questions and get answers. (Respect but don't be intimidated by professionals, such as lawyers or doctors.) Whatever advice you do get and from whomever, think about it and decide for yourself if it's right or best *for you*.

151

Get your priorities straight and *prioritize your life*. This means acknowledging tasks and goals that will provide the most value or benefit (now and in the future) and doing them before doing other things. Your priorities should include: health, fitness, exercise and personal growth (learning). They should also include: time with family and true friends, things that will provide financial security in the future (investments and your own home, for instance), and of course, happiness, yours and of those you care about.

152

No matter how many times or how often you get knocked down (make mistakes or experience setbacks in life) – *get right back up*. No excuses, no complaining and no blaming others – just get up. Each time you get knocked down, get up and *determine why* you were knocked down. Then do something, anything positive, to prevent or reduce the chances of the why from happening again. We all get knocked down. Those who get back up get what they want. Thomas Edison, Walt Disney, Bill Gates, Oprah Winfrey, Steven Spielberg, J.K. Rowling and many others got up when they were knocked down.

153

Life isn't fair or unfair, it's just life. Feeling that life is unfair or that you got a raw deal isn't going to make things better. It will, however, put you in the wrong mindset (negative). This will stop you from doing what needs to be done to deal with or overcome what you feel is unfair. If you can't seem to shake off the feeling that your life isn't fair, take a minute to think about those who are far less fortunate than you.

I cried because I had no shoes until I met a man who had no feet. (Anonymous)

154

Better be wise by the misfortunes of others than by your own.[30] Simply by observing the mistakes and misfortunes of other people, we can greatly reduce life's learning curve. We can save ourselves time, energy, money, stress, heartache and even our life having to learn or experience those things for ourselves. Talk with and read about people who have tried to do but were unsuccessful in doing the things that you want to do. Learn from their failure (how not to do it or how they wish they had done it). This may help you to succeed in doing it. Also talk with and read about those who tried and did succeed.

155

In the end, it's not the years in your life that count. It's the life in your years.[31] Chances are when we reach the end of our life, we will regret not doing the things we wished we had done. Live your life – fill your life with experiences. Set and achieve goals, travel, volunteer, try new things, do things with family and friends, and do the things you truly enjoy doing as often as you can. Don't wait for *someday* or until you *have the time*. That day or time might never come. Fill your life with life every day.

156

We can learn from our mistakes, miscalculations and bad decisions, but some are better not made. One mistake, one miscalculation, one bad decision or simple carelessness could ruin your life. Think before you act. Stop before you react. Before you act or react, ask yourself if doing what you are about to do will help you to get closer to being who you truly wish to be and getting what you really want in life. If it won't, don't. It might take a second or two to think before you act. It's likely to take a lot of self-control not to react. But doing so could save you from messing up your life.

157

Be careful what you do and how you spend your time. Once something has been done, it can't be undone. It happened, it's part of the past. For instance, cheating on your partner. Things with your partner will never be the way they were. You *might* be able to do something to mend hurt feelings or rebuild trust, but things will *never* be the same. Same with time, once spent, it's part of the past. There's *nothing you can do* to get it back. Constantly checking emails, for instance. Time lost, time that could have been used *productively*.

158

Be independent. This doesn't mean being single or a loner. It means not feeling a need for another person in order to be happy, confident or feel complete. It's about being able to be who you really are. It means thinking for yourself and making your own choices and decisions. It's about knowing that you are able to do and get what you need or want when you need or want to do it or have it. When you are independent, you – feel good about yourself when alone with yourself, decide who and what you wish to be and do, make money doing what you enjoy doing and live *your life* how you wish to live it.

159

Everything we hear is an opinion, not a fact. Everything we see is a perspective, not the truth.[32] (Almost everything.) A lot of what we hear (what others say) are people's beliefs, opinion, lies or agenda. All of what people see is their own perspective. Culture, bias, upbringing, experiences, openness or lack of and intent or purpose influence what people say, hear and see. With so much false or misleading information and propaganda floating around, for a better you and life, question what you hear and be careful of what you believe. Look for and use the facts and truth.

160

If you (your brain) think that things in yourself or in your life are OK or are the best they can be when they aren't, your brain will stop you from changing those things. For instance, if you think that you will always live an average life, you won't do anything to create and live an exceptional life. To *make changes* isn't always easy but it's simple. You simply need to take an objective look at yourself and at your life and *acknowledge* (think) what you need and want to change. Then force yourself to do whatever needs to be done that will enable you to make those changes.

161

People of accomplishment rarely sat back and let things happen to them. They went out and happened to things.[33] We need to be proactive (plan, anticipate and act) in order to acquire and accomplish what we want in life. This means that we need to set realistic goals and create realistic strategies to get and achieve whatever it may be. It means that we can't procrastinate and that we must be persistent – keep doing what we need to do to get what we want. It also means that we need to reduce or eliminate distractions so that we can use our time and energy to *make things happen*.

162

Teachers open the door, but you must enter by yourself.[34] Teachers can teach us but only we can learn from what they teach. It's up to us to listen carefully and to ask questions until we understand. It's up to us to decide whether what they have taught will benefit us and to put into practice the things that will. *Teachers* are all around us – in our relationships (parents, partners, friends), people we don't know or may not even like, and at work and in places we have never been (foreign countries, for instance). We need to recognize them and learn from them what we can.

163

Next to health, time is our second most valuable asset. We cannot buy more time nor can we do anything without it. What we do with our time, how we use it, will determine what we get in life. Waste it and get little or nothing at all. We need to limit or eliminate time wasters, such as, time spent on our phone, computer, tablet, social media sites and blogs. We need to spend less time, for instance: with people who aren't really our friends, watching TV, and commuting to and from work. (Working from home or finding a job closer to home can save hours every week.)

164

Actions speak louder than words.[35] What we do is more important than what we say. Action *shows* others what we think and feel. It shows truth in what we would *otherwise* say. It builds trust and confidence in others about us and proves that we mean and do what we say. For instance, in a relationship in which you do something from time to time that annoys the other person: saying "Sorry" is merely a word to say. Whereas, if you stop doing what you do that annoys the other person (action), it shows them that you know it annoys them and that you are sorry.

165

Life is *unpredictable*. We need to accept this and to be prepared for the unpredictable. We need a plan. Although a plan may not prevent an unpredictable event from occurring, it can minimize the consequences of what happens if it does happen. If we lost our job, for instance. An *acted on* plan to have money saved to support us until we got another job will make things easier. At the same time, we shouldn't think or worry too much about what may happen, as doing so can create unnecessary stress. In fact, by doing so, our subconscious might actually make it happen.

166

Remember when life's path is steep, keep your mind even.[36] When life is tough or is not the way you want it to be, don't allow your emotions to take control. *Losing control* of our emotions will have a negative effect on our judgment. This can lead us to react (do something in response to anger, for instance) rather than act (deal with or fix the things that aren't the way we would like them to be). It's OK to be emotional, just don't lose control of your emotions. When we're in control, we are in a much better place to rationally deal with, fix or improve whatever it may be.

167

Start and do the important things in life early in your life. For instance, take care of your health from the day you understand the meaning of health. Get the right education as soon as you determine the education you will need in order to get what you want in life. Travel overseas before life gets so busy that you don't have the time to travel. Find a career that you truly enjoy or create and start your own business as soon as you have the knowledge and skills you will need to start it and make it work. Save and invest as soon as you start making money. And love and be loved the moment you know what love is.

168

If you do not change direction, you may end up where you are heading.[37] If you don't do something to change the things in your life that aren't the way you wish things to be, chances are life may take you where you probably don't want to be. Take the time to consider – *what would I change in myself and in my life so far if I could change it?* Would it be: having more savings, more investments, a better education, different friends, or maybe live in a different city or country. After you do, focus on changing those things in yourself and in your life now, before it's too late.

169

Don't stand by the water and long for fish; go home and weave a net.[38] Actions create outcomes. Without action there is no outcome. We cannot simply sit around waiting for things to happen the way we want things to happen. We can't expect other people to make the things we want happen. We need to plan, anticipate, initiate, do and follow through. We must have the things we need (for instance, knowledge, skills, time, motivation and control of the actions we need to take) to do what must be done to get the outcomes (results) we need and desire.

170

Your life *depends on* your choices, decisions, actions and reactions. Every choice, decision, action and reaction we make or take has a consequence, which will determine who we are, who we will become and the life we live. We (almost always) have the power to: have a choice, make or change our decision, and decide to act rather than react to the things that happen to us. People, the media and our emotions can cloud our judgment and influence our choices, decisions, actions and reactions. Do not allow people, the media or your emotions to take this power away.

171

What isn't started today is never finished tomorrow.[39]
Who we are and the life we live today is mainly the result of all the things we started and finished on our yesterdays. It's also a result of the things we never started or never finished. If you are not where you want to be in your life today, chances are it's because you didn't start and finish what you needed to start and finish to be there. Get started today. Do something, no matter how small. Regularly review what you're doing to ensure that it will get you where you want to be. If it will – don't stop until it's finished.

172

A small change in yourself or in your life can lead to big changes in your life. Make a change. Read more. Be more positive. Save a little more. Try new and different things. Change the way you do things. Learn a new skill. Look for and create opportunities that will enable you to do more and experience more. Meet new people. Change your job. Travel the world. Make more time by wasting less time. Get fit. Change a habit or two. Move to a new/better environment (city, state or country). Create and achieve new goals. Change things to change your life.

173

Goals are the blueprints to our future. We need goals – daily, one week, one month, six month, one year, five year and even ten year goals – to really live life. When achieved, goals enable us to create and live our life the way we wish to live it. They enable us to focus our time and energy on things that are important and worthwhile to us. When we achieve our goals, our self-esteem and self-confidence get a boost. This encourages us to set and achieve more goals, thus getting more of what we need and want in life.

174

The greater danger for most of us lies not in setting our aim too high and falling short; but in setting our aim too low, and achieving our mark.[40] Our self-confidence determines what we expect we will get. When we expect less, we usually get less. When we expect more, we usually get more. The only thing that stops you from achieving great things in life is you. You need to believe that you can achieve great things in life. (You can.) Set goals that are a little beyond your expectations. Create and put into action effective plans and strategies that will enable you to achieve those goals. Each one achieved encourages us to achieve more.

175

People who truly excel in life are those who take *full responsibility for and maximum control* of their life. They make their own choices and decisions, act based on their definitions, rules, standards, beliefs and values, and are accountable for the actions they take. They don't sit and wait, they take action. They don't make excuses or blame others when things don't go the way they had planned, they look to themselves. When goals cannot be reached, they don't give up on their goals, they adjust or change their *how-to achieve* method or strategies so they can achieve them.

176

To get what you want in life, you cannot allow failure to stop you from getting it. You will fail sometimes, possible many times, to get what you want. We all do. When we do fail, we need to believe that if we gave it our utmost effort, it's not us who failed, it's the method we used that failed. We then need to determine why it failed so that we can find a better method and *do it* again. If we allow it, failure can have a negative effect on our *self-esteem* and *self-confidence*, believing that we don't deserve to or can't get it. This will definitely stop us from getting it.

177

Expect setbacks in life. Things will happen and may happen when you least expect it. Don't feel hopeless or stuck and don't give up on yourself when setbacks do happen. Acknowledge your feelings (disappointment). Learn what you can and stay positive. Regain control of the aspects of the task, goal or situation that you can control (which often is most). Then, as soon as possible, redirect your focus to moving forward; staying focused on creating options and taking action that will enable you to overcome the setback.

178

Great things are done by a series of small things brought together.[41] We can achieve great things in life by breaking up the things we wish to achieve into a series of small tasks or projects. This helps us to remain motivated and determined to do what needs to be done, as each of the individual small tasks or projects require less time and effort than it would to take on the whole task or project. This works well with *large goals*. The goal is broken into a series of mini goals. When we achieve each mini goal, we *reward* ourselves. We then move onto the next one until all of the mini goals are achieved; brought together as one.

179

Life is full of problems. Worrying about those problems won't fix, change or eliminate them. It won't make us feel better either. To handle life's problems, we need to determine what we can control and use that control to deal with those problems. We also need to be prepared for things we can't control by maintaining a *positive attitude* (which will give us control of how we act or react to those problems). A lot of what we worry will happen, often doesn't happen. Most of the things that do happen usually have solutions. Rather than waste time worrying about problems, use the time to find solutions.

180

If you aren't honest with yourself, your life is certain to be a drag. Tell yourself the truth. If you aren't happy with yourself, tell yourself that you aren't and do something to change who you are. If you don't like your job, tell yourself that you don't and do something to get a better job. If you don't really like the people you hang out with, tell yourself that you don't and look for different people to hang with. If you don't like the person you live with, tell yourself it's time to find someone else and find that person.

181

Trying is not enough. To try means to *attempt to*, with an implied meaning that we might not succeed. Neither is telling yourself that you're doing your best. If you aren't getting closer to being who you wish to be or aren't getting what you want in life, you aren't doing your best. When we say *I'll try*, our brain can set us up for failure, as not succeeding is a possible outcome within the meaning of "to try". Instead, tell yourself (and believe it) that you *must do it*. When we must do something, we give it our best and get it done.

182

It is impossible to begin to learn that which one thinks one already knows.[42] Thinking that we already know something (when we don't) prevents us from knowing what we don't know. Thinking that we already know something can result in our ignoring or refusing to listen to and consider suggestions or advice from others. All of this can stop us from learning the truth, new things or new ways to do things. Be smart – know that you don't know it all and recognize that what others know might be what you need to know to make your life easier and happier, and enable you to get more of what you want in life.

183

Unless you do something beyond what you have already mastered, you will never grow.[43] To get the most out of life, we need to grow. To grow we need to stretch ourselves; to do more, learn more and experience new things. We need to step outside our comfort zone, take (*calculated*) risks, take on challenges, find, create and act on opportunities and set and achieve goals. You don't need to wait to master something before you do something beyond what you've mastered. Do something (many things) beyond what you're already *good at* – so that you are certain to grow.

184

Nothing is worth more than this day.[44] Yesterday is gone. Tomorrow might never come. Today is the day to be happy and to do the things you enjoy doing. Today is the day to spend quality time with family and true friends. It's the day to start new projects and to finish old ones. It's the day to be good to people and to help people who need a helping hand. Today is the day to laugh and the day to truly enjoy and experience living. Live life today. Don't put it off until tomorrow. If you do, you might never live it.

185

It's quality rather than quantity that matters.[45] Quality rather than quantity matters in everything in life. Quality not quantity determines whether we are truly happy in life. Quality friends (a few *real friends*) are far more valuable than a lot of so-called friends. Quality sex one day a week is far more gratifying than second-rate sex every day of the week. Thirty minutes of quality (productive) time is worth far more than three hours of idle time. One pound of quality food is far better than five pounds of junk food. 70 years of good health is far happier and more enjoyable than 100 years of poor health….

186

Go confidently in the direction of your dreams. Live the life you have imagined.[46] Our dreams (hopes and desires) are our conscious thoughts and visions of who and what we wish to become and what we wish to do in and with our life. These dreams can lead us to create goals to achieve. These goals (dreams), if achieved, can become our reality. Take the time to dream and be creative when you dream. Develop the confidence to follow those dreams (to make them happen) so that you can live the life of your dreams.

187

Do not go where the path may lead, go instead where there is no path and leave a trail.[47] Life provides us all with an opportunity to create and live a special and unique life (our life). This opportunity can enable us to do or create something that has never been done or created before. Doing as others do, following the path that others are on or have traveled, is likely to get us what others will or have gotten in life (their life). Trust yourself to *create your own path*, to be an innovator rather than an imitator.

188

First say to yourself what would you be; and then do what you have to do.[48] One of the hardest things in life may be deciding who we truly wish to be and what we genuinely want to do in life. Take the time and make the effort to discover who and what that is. This will enable you to determine what you must do to become who and to get what you truly want. Knowing that, you can then start to take action to get what you desire. To get started, don't think about what you don't want. Doing so may lead your *subconscious mind* to concentrate on those things, possibly making the things you don't want – happen.

189

The wise make more opportunities than they find.[49] Opportunities can enable us to fix, improve, add or eliminate pretty much anything and everything in every aspect of our being and our life. We can make our own opportunities. This means that our opportunities are almost infinite. Opportunity is about timing. If we wait for opportunities, we may not be ready to act on them. When we make our own opportunities, we can ensure that the timing will be right for us to act, thus getting more of what we really want in life.

190

To become who we truly wish to be and to create and live the life we really want to live, we need to:

- Believe that we deserve to (*self-esteem*)
- Feel that we are able to (*self-confidence*) and
- Think that we can (*positive attitude*).

To give yourself the best chance of getting what you truly desire in life, do whatever you need to do to:

- Improve your *self-esteem* and *self-confidence*.
- Develop and maintain a *positive attitude*.

191

Question what you believe. Rather than look for information that supports what you currently believe to be correct, look for information that proves that what you believe is *wrong*. Our brain has the tendency to look for, give more importance or relevance to, and accept information that confirms or supports what we already believe (*bias confirmation*). This bias means that we may unconsciously discount or ignore information that's contrary to or critical of what we believe, information that may provide evidence that what we believe is flawed or even incorrect.

192

That some achieve great success is proof to all that others can achieve it as well.[50] Seeing is believing. To see someone achieve something is proof that something can be done. This can provide us the motivation we need to set out to do and achieve the same, and more. The four minute mile was thought to be impossible, until it was achieved in 1954. Since then, others have done the same; one person running it in 3 minutes 43 seconds. Spend time with people who have succeeded in achieving what you wish to achieve in your life. Observe, ask questions, listen, learn and act.

193

Emotional intelligence may be more important than IQ. Emotional intelligence includes things like: (1) knowing and understanding our emotions, (2) recognizing their impact on ourselves and on others, (3) managing our emotions so to get along with other people and to lead to mutually satisfying benefits, (4) taking others' feelings into account when interacting with them, and (5) adapting to circumstances and situations as they change. Being emotional intelligent is certain to make life happier and healthier. Take the time to understand and improve your emotional intelligence. It will make a difference in your life.

194

When one door closes another opens; but we often look so long and so regretfully upon the closed door that we do not see the one which has opened for us.[51] Some opportunities might only be available for a few days, hours, minutes or maybe just a few seconds. The ones we miss may be the ones that could have enabled us to make positive changes in ourselves and in our life. We need to quickly accept those that we missed and remain in control of our emotions so that we can be ready and waiting to recognize and act on the next one.

195

It does not matter how slowly you go as long as you do not stop.[52] To get what we want in life requires desire, enthusiasm, action and perseverance. We need to truly desire what we tell ourselves we want. We need to be genuinely passionate and excited about getting what we want in order to motivate ourselves to do what we need to do to get it. We must take action. We cannot settle for less than what we desire. And, importantly, we need to keep doing what we need to do to get what we want until we do get it.

196

Getting what you want in life isn't always easy but it's simple. Simply do whatever it takes, no matter how large or small, to get it. For instance, when you have a thought, idea or feeling that might help you to get what you want, do something *physical* within a few seconds of having it. That may be as simple as writing down an idea on a piece of paper. Doing something straight-away keeps the thought, idea or feeling alive, to continue to be acted on. Doing nothing is likely to result in that thought, idea or feeling being forgotten and never acted on – something that may have helped to make your life better.

197

There is nothing like a daydream to create the future.[53] A daydream (mental wandering) is an experience that takes place when we consciously have lost focus on what we are doing, allowing our mind to wander. When in this zone, we forget about our current reality and let our imagination run wild. It's a *time and place* where we can: think outside the box, create new ideas and visualize our future. Take the time to sit in a quiet and peaceful place, and daydream. What you dream may help you to create the future you desire.

198

You can miss a lot of life if you are too busy in life. *Stop and smell the roses*. Take the time to truly appreciate and experience life. Stop and look at the night sky and watch the sun rise. Smell the flowers in your garden or when walking in nature. Pause to truly taste the food you eat. Spend time with family and real friends. Do the things you enjoy doing and go to the places you wish to go. Be happy with and grateful for what you have now while you are working toward getting what you want in the future. And make the time to do the important things in life (such as, getting enough sleep, nutrition and exercise).

199

Do whatever you do – right the first time. It can be painful, can take you longer, can even cost you more, to fix or undo what *wasn't* done right the first time. Conditions or the situation could change that may make it impossible to fix what needs fixing. Conditions or the situation could change that might prevent you from undoing what needs to be undone. Take the time to know the right way to do something *before* setting out to do it. For instance, before building a fence or getting married, know what you are in for; the time and things you need in order to do it right.

200

Never stop learning. The one thing you should have learned by the time you graduated or will graduate from school is that most, if not all, of what they taught you in school is not going to get you what you need or really want in life. If it did, everyone who graduated from school would have everything they need and truly want in life. Take it upon yourself (*self-study*) to learn what you need to know that will enable you to become who you truly wish to be living life the way you really want to live it. (Having read this book is a great start. ☺)

201 (Epilogue)

You must have a goal, a clear vision of where you want to go in your life. If you don't know where that is, you'll never get there. If you wait for life to turn out the way you want it to turn out, it won't. You need to have a clear vision of who you wish to be and what you want in life so that you can take action to make it happen.

Part of that vision *needs to* include how you want your life to be when you're old. (One day you will be, and that day will be sooner than you think.) This is something that you need to think about, plan for and start doing something about when you're in your 20s, 30s, 40s and 50s. (You might take a few minutes to think about it every year on your birthday and ask yourself if your plans and goals and your actions are still on target to enable you to be healthy, happy and financially secure when you are old.)

Don't merely live life, do something exceptional in and with your life. Don't be ordinary, be extraordinary. Be a good and kind person and be great at whatever you decide to do. You don't have to be the best, just be great at what you do. And aim to do or create something that helps to make the world a better place.

You have the opportunity to become who you truly wish to be and to live your whole life the way you can dream of living it. Ask more, read more, learn more and create ways that will enable you to do so. Once you know what you need to know to make it all happen, focus on it, give it your utmost attention and don't stop until it happens. You'll be so happy that you did.

Have a great life.

If you enjoyed this book, your review on your favorite book-seller's website or a nice comment on Facebook or other social media sites or blogs would certainly be most appreciated.

BONUS

For 40 More Things You Need to Know

Go to Page 133

More from Simple Logic Publications.

Ever wonder if *you might be a Dickhead*? Maybe you aren't really sure what makes someone a Dickhead. Or maybe you aren't a Dickhead but you know someone who is, someone who does not know that they are in fact a Dickhead, and you want them to know that they are.

If so, this book is for you.

Are You A Dickhead? asks the reader 100 simple questions and provides simple multiple choice answers. By answering the questions, the reader is able to generate a score. This score enables the reader to determine if they are or are not in fact a Dickhead.

From inside *Are You A Dickhead?*

When in public, do you: (Question 1)

R   Pick your nose and look at what you picked.
U   Pick your nose and flick whatever you picked out into the air.
A   Pick your nose only when you know for sure that no one is looking or watching.
D   Pick your nose and eat what you have picked out.
H   Pick your nose and put what you picked out into your pocket to eat later.

When riding on a plane, train, bus or subway, do you: (Question 34)

R   Stink (have BO) or reek of garlic.
U   Allow your body to lean onto someone you don't know who is seated next to you.
A   Fall asleep on the shoulder of someone you don't know who is sitting next to you.
D   Sit with your mouth wide open, snore or drool, or all of the above.
H   Smell kind of nice, allow the person sitting next to you to have and use their space by keeping your body parts in your part of your seat, and always ensure that your mouth doesn't hang open and that you don't snore or drool.

Things to Read

Do the people you think are *friends* do or fail to do things that you expect a friend to not do or to do? Does it seem like they have forgotten what it means to be a *friend*? Or could it be that they don't have a clue what it takes to be a friend?

Do some of your *friends* get irritated, even upset with you for things you do or don't do? Could it be that you have forgotten or don't really know what it means or takes to be a friend?

If so, this book is for them, and you.

This book takes a *fun but serious* look at 100 things real friends do and don't do. It looks at things that make someone a real friend, things such as: accepting us for who we really are, and telling us if we have a booger hanging out of our nose – when we do.

From inside *What Friends SHOULD Do*

Friends tell their friends if they have a big honking zit on their face. (No. 1)

The same applies to boogers hanging out of our nose, bad breath, body odor and things stuck in between our teeth or hanging out of our mouth. A real friend wouldn't let their friend walk around all day or night wondering why people are looking at or pointing at them – unaware of any freaky or smelly stuff that is sticking out of or coming from their body. A real friend will let us know immediately if they notice something that needs our attention (things like zits, boogers, or B.O.).

Friends help friends find solutions to their problems. (No. 29)

A real friend is there and ready to help a friend with a problem. It may be a problem a friend recognizes on their own. Or it might be something a friend sees in a friend that the friend doesn't see themselves. Either way, a real friend doesn't attack a friend with nasty comments but rather *attacks the problem* (helps find a solution). A real friend is only interested in helping their friend work out their problem. For instance: if a friend is really overweight, a real friend doesn't call that friend gigantor or chunky. A real friend would organize time with that friend to exercise together, to lose weight. If a friend loses their job, a real friend won't call the friend a loser. A real friend helps their friend to determine why they lost their job and what they can do to get another job.

Things to Read

When your daughter was born, you probably thought about, may have even dreamed about, the kind of man that she would (you hoped her to) marry. That perfect man, the man who you would be proud of – your Son-In-Law.

That wonderful day finally arrives. Your daughter gets married. But to your horror, disapproval and disappointment, your daughter married a loser, an idiot, a real dickhead, someone you truly despise. From that day forward, you might had thought all was lost, that there was nothing you could do.

This happened to me, and that's what I thought.

Over the months and years that followed, I thought about and later put into action 100 things that enabled me to get my revenge. All 100 are in this book.

From inside *I Hate My Son-In Law*

Here are a few of the things I did to my son-in-law:

- ✔ No. 1 I used his toothbrush to clean the bathroom sink drain hole.

- ✔ No 16 I stuck my finger down my throat and barfed all over the hood of his car.

- ✔ No. 21 I put some fresh dog poop in his jacket pocket.

- ✔ No. 40 I farted on his pillow, more than once.

- ✔ No. 85 I ordered Suzy the sex doll for him, to be delivered to his home while he was at work and his wife (my daughter) was sure to be home.

Disclaimer: The book *I Hate My Son-In Law* is sold with the full understanding that the authors and publisher **shall not be held liable or responsible** to any person or entity in any way with respect to, including but not limited to, any physical, psychological, emotional, commercial or financial (including business or employment) loss, injury, damage or costs or any interference, damage or loss to any current or future relationship incidentally or consequentially directly or indirectly caused, or alleged to have been caused, by anything contained within or in connection with this book or any of its content whatsoever.

Things to Read

Life 101 (the series) will be available in 2023.

Have you ever wondered why you think, believe and do the things you do? Have you ever thought about why you like the things you like and buy the things you buy. Ever consider why you deal with the things that happen to you how you do or why you treat people the way you do?

Understanding why can help you to take control of yourself and your life. Doing so enables you to become who and do what you really want in life.

This book looks at:

- Our Subconscious Mind – How it can work for and against us
- Influences in our Life – How they affect who we are and become and what we do
- Peer Pressure – Its effect on us
- The Media, Marketing and Advertising – How it all messes with our mind and our life

124 201 Things You Need to Know About Life

If someone were to ask you, *Who are you?* what would you tell them? Would you tell them where you work or what you do to earn a living? Would you tell them that you are single, married or divorced and that you have 2 children and a dog? Would you also tell them where you live or what your partner does? All of it may be true, but these things aren't who you are.

This book looks at:

- Masks – masks we wear and hide behind

- Perception – where it comes from and how it affects us

- Definitions, Rules, Standards – what things mean to us and where we draw the line

- Beliefs and Values – what we hold to be true and what's truly important to us

- Attitude – the impact it has on who we are, what we do, how we do it and why we do it

Have you ever wondered why some people seem to cruise though life effortlessly; seeming to get everything they want? They have a fantastic partner, cool friends, good health, great job, an amazing house, and vacations in exotic countries; everything they want in life, just like in the movies.

It's often simple things that enable some people to get the life they really want and stop others from doing so. It's often these simple things that some people *may be allowing* to stop them from living their dreams.

This book looks at:

- The Need to Know Who You Really Are
- Time
- Mind Games
- Pride
- Other Simple Things – Things that can stop us from living the life we could be living

Some of the things that are stopping you from getting what you really want in life aren't so simple. However, once they have been recognized, all can be dealt with so that they can't or will no longer stop you from getting and living the life you really want to live.

This book looks at:

- Fear
- Habits
- Memories
- Procrastination
- Motivation and Determination
- Six More Not-So-Simple Things

How we feel about ourselves (our *self-esteem* and *self-confidence)* can either stop us from getting what we want in life, or empower us to drive ourselves to become who we really want to be and enable us to get the life of our dreams. What we think about ourselves determines who we are and who we become. And whether we believe that we have what it takes to get what we want determines what we can get in life.

How and what we feel about ourselves and our abilities will determine whether we will have what it takes to do what we need to do to make changes in ourselves and in our life. It's self-esteem and self-confidence that can enable us to turn our life around by putting us on our chosen path, one that will get us what we want in life.

This book looks at:

- Self-Esteem
- Self-Confidence

TAKE RESPONSIBILITY FOR YOUR LIFE

6

People who truly excel in what they do in life, are those who take full responsibility for and maximum control of their life. Many might have had coaches, trainers or advisers who helped them to maximize their true strengths and talents, but the person who excels *makes the choice to do so*. Those who do are the one who decides to put in the time and effort that's required to get what they want. They take both the credit and the blame for what they do and what they get and don't get in life. They take action and get things done to make it all happen the way they want it to happen.

This book looks at:

- What responsibility means
- What could stop us from being in control
- Having the right attitude
- Benefits and rewards for taking responsibility

Things to Read

The saddest thing in life may be not knowing who we want to be and what we want to do in our life. If we don't know *who we are*, we won't know what we need to do to become who we truly want to be. If we don't know who we want to be, we won't know what to do with our life. If we don't know what to do in and with our life, we could end up wasting our life being someone we aren't doing something we don't really want to do in and with our life. To live a truly happy and satisfying life, we need to discover and be who we want to be doing what we want to do in and with our life.

This book looks at:

- Self-Discovery
- Self-Assessment – to determine what we need to change to be and get what we want
- The Payoff – the real benefits and rewards of knowing our true self

If we don't know how to make the right choices and decisions for us, we won't get what we truly want in life. If we don't make our own choices and decisions, other people may try to make them for us. This is likely to mean that what we get is what they want, not necessarily what we want in life.

We all have the ability to choose and decide for ourselves. It may be that we choose and decide to be with different people. Maybe we choose and decide to work and live in a different city, state or country where things are better for us, where things are the way we want things to be. Or it may be that we decide to better ourselves, to do something different or to create something new.

This book looks at:

- Choices and Decisions and How to Make Them
- Things That Influence Choices and Decisions
- The Cost of Making Decisions

Things to Read

Everything we want or create in our life begins as a thought, an abstract idea that can fulfill a need or want. These *ideas* can later become goals, objectives or plans that we may decide to act on and strive to achieve, enabling us to get *what we desire*.

Goals can help us to change anything and everything in our life. They can enable us to move forward in our life, to become who we want to be and get what we want when we want it. Goals can make life more exciting and interesting. The right goals, when achieved, can lead to amazing results, outcomes, benefits and rewards.

This book looks at:

- Why We Need Goals
- Discovering Our Goals
- Setting Our Goals
- Achieving Our Goals

132 201 Things You Need to Know About Life

If things aren't working in your life or they aren't the way you had hoped they would be, something needs to change. If you don't like who you are or what you are doing in or with your life now, you need to change the way things are. If you keep getting the same results and outcomes, results and outcomes you don't want, it's time for change. If where you are heading in life isn't where you want to go, you need to change your direction.

This book looks at:

- Change
- Attitude
- Pain and Pleasure
- Opportunity
- Being Proactive
- How to Make Changes
- How to Make Things Happen

40 More Things You Need To Know

1. It's great to be different. Be different. Be great.

2. Your attitude and personality will always be far more important than your looks and the clothes, makeup and jewelry you wear.

3. Don't think you have to be right all the time. You don't need to be. Besides, you never will be.

4. To get where you want to go in your working life, you need connections. You need to get out and make those connections (network) even if you hate doing it. Learn how to do it right and do it.

5. In life, no one owes you anything, not even your parents. You and only you are responsible for what you get in your life.

6. Don't burn your bridges. In other words, don't end a relationship (personal, work or project) in such a way that you would likely never be able to go back or re-start the relationship. Exceptions may be: when it's in your best interest not to go back to that relationship (domestic violence, for instance), to protect your reputation, or to help a true friend.

7. Stop sleeping in. You'll get plenty of sleep when you're dead. After 7–8 hours of quality sleep, get

up and do something productive toward getting what you truly want in life.

8. There are some crazy (literally insane) people out there. Learn how to *recognize* them, then avoid them and know when to get away from them.

9. Believe in yourself. If you don't currently, you need to do what needs to be done to improve your self-esteem and self-confidence.

10. Not everyone is going to like you. No biggie.

11. Good manners go a long way in any country. Practice good manners in and outside your home. And before you travel, learn a little about the local customs (manners) of the country you will visit.

12. Learn to be patient. Good things come to those who are patient.

13. We all need time for ourselves. A hobby that we can do on our own is a great time to spend with ourselves.

14. Read every day, even if only one page. (Bet you can't read just one.) In a year, you could read that 365 pages book you've always wanted to read but the mere size of it has put you off for years.

15. Quitting or losing your job or breaking up with a boyfriend/girlfriend can be the best thing to ever happen to you. A better job or someone better is

out there. Rather than cry or sulk, determine why it happened (what wasn't right for you) and find a job or person that works better for you.

16. The older you get the easier it is to gain weight and harder it is to lose it.

17. It's much harder and takes longer to get out of debt than it is to get into debt.

18. A university degree doesn't guarantee that you will be rich or successful. It also doesn't mean that you will get a good job or one that you like.

19. Beware of student loans. They are likely to put you in serious debt for a long time (years).

20. One of the best things you can do early in your career is to concentrate on increasing your earning potential rather than on increasing how much you earn.

21. Write things down. Put a pen and pad of paper next to your bed. Great ideas that could change your life can come to you just before falling asleep or even wake you up during your sleep. Write them down. If you don't, you'll very likely forget them when you wake up in the morning.

↓ 22-40 SEX ↓

It's your choice and decision what you do regarding sex, but consider this:

22. It's OK to do it with *yourself* (masturbate) if there is no one who wants to do it with you or no one you really want to do it with. Touching yourself (in moderation) is a normal and healthy sexual activity. Doing it can: help you to learn what you like – to show and share with your next sex partner, improve your sexual endurance for the next time you have sex with another person, and it should make you feel really good.

23. Many people masturbate (girls and guys) even if they say that they don't. More than you probably think. Doing it (masturbating) isn't weird or to be ashamed of, unless you do it all day, do in public places, doing it prevents you from having a normal sex life with another human being when the opportunity comes up, or it prevents you from living a healthy, happy life.

24. Masturbation won't make you go blind, your eyes won't fall out, your dick won't fall off, you won't go crazy and you aren't a bad person.

25. You don't need to have sex to be cool. Most people in school who talk about having a lot of sex, aren't. They are lying. Chances are they never have had sex with a real person.

26. It's not a race to lose your virginity. Memories of the *first time* are greater if you lost it somewhere and with someone special rather than in the back

40 More Things

of an old crusty Ford van with a freak or weirdo. (If it will be your first time, before you do, watch the movie *Fast Times at Ridgement High* (1982).)

27. Don't have sex to get a guy to like you. Chances are he will dump you soon after he humps you.

28. Exploring and experimentation is great but do not get pressured into doing something you aren't comfortable doing. Trust your instincts. If your first instinct says No, say No and don't do it.

29. You can always change your mind. Tell him or her if you don't want to do it. Or tell him or her to stop if you don't like what he or she is doing, even if in the middle of sex.

30. Guys – The size of your penis might matter to *some women* but apparently the majority of women don't seem to really care. For most women, how a guy uses it and the kind of guy behind it is more important than its size. Pulling on, hanging a heavy rock from or using an odd looking pump will not get you a bigger dick.

31. Girls – Never tell a guy that he has a small dick. Most guys are *super sensitive* about the size of their penis, even if theirs is average sized. (Apparently, the average adult penis is about 5.2 inches (13.2 cm) in length when hard). Guys and girls, simply live with what you have got or get, learn how to use it and have fun.

32. Guys – *Always ask* her before touching her special parts (goodies) and know that *No* means No.

33. Foreplay – Learn what your partner likes and keep it slow. The longer the better but do move forward when the time is right for your partner. He or she will likely let you know when. A few seconds or minutes is *never* enough. Become a master and you will be rewarded.

34. You have heard it before. But here it is again. Always have safe sex. Use a condom. A balloon or plastic baggy will not do the trick. Neither will a rubber band or a douche. An unwanted pregnancy can really mess up your future plans. A sexually transmitted disease can give you a bad reputation, can make you ill or at least send you to the doctor, and if it's AIDS, it may even kill you.

35. Guys – You might think it is or want it to be but sex isn't over when you have an orgasm. It's not time to roll over and fall asleep or to turn on the TV or your phone or computer. It's time to ensure that she get the pleasure she deserves. Lie down together, touch her, use a toy, talk with her and ask her what she wants and give it to her. Don't accept *It's OK* or *I'm OK* if she isn't.

36. Girls – Don't fake it. If you do, you may never get it. If you don't get what you want, tell your partner that you didn't and show him or her what you need to have an orgasm.

37. Girls – Most guys are horny – almost all of the time. They would love to touch and squeeze your goodies if you drop your guard.

38. Alcohol and drugs reduce your guard. If you don't want someone touching, squeezing or playing with your body, don't put yourself in places or situations where drunk or stoned guys or girls are around (especially if you are or intend to get drunk or stoned).

39. If you know that the person you are having sex with is cheating on someone else as you are having sex with them, chances are that they will one day cheat on you too.

For those new or kind of new to sex:

40. Don't expect or judge your or your partner's performance based on Hollywood or pornographic movies. What goes in, what comes out and how long it lasts in those movies is pure fantasy. Reality is, what goes in is likely an average sized penis, what comes out will be about a teaspoonful, it's likely to last only a few minutes and it will probably be a bit disappointing. The good news is, with practice and with the right people, it's going to get better (much better) and will last longer.

It's not whether you win or lose, it's knowing that you gave it your best and all.

www.ingramcontent.com/pod-product-compliance
Lightning Source LLC
Chambersburg PA
CBHW070613010526
44118CB00012B/1497